CRAIG AND HIS JOURNEY TOWARDS CHRIST

CRAIG AND HIS JOURNEY TOWARDS CHRIST

My encounter with the true author of life

Craig Harrison

To order additional copies of this book, contact:
Xlibris Corporation
0-800-644-6988
www.xlibrispublishing.co.uk
Orders@xlibrispublishing.co.uk
302478

Contents

Prologue

I am Craig Harrison and I am not ashamed to say "I have God in my life." Ever since the Lord stepped into my existence I have begun to change for the better, He has cured me of alcoholism and all the mental health problems it causes; Thank you Lord; nowadays I look at the world from another level.

It is my belief that the circle of life I once took for granted is diminishing by the day. I believe the future of the world's prosperity is being threatened by the greediness of mankind. Corporate greed and that by those in authority, upsets the balance of planet earth, wildlife and civilisation. I consider I have to look in the mirror and transform my own ways, and start to play it Mother Nature's way or she will take it all away. I play it God's way nowadays. We can change the world by one act of random kindness at time. It's so simple Jesus commanded us how to live in the holy gospel, I take heed to His word and it truly works, praise the Lord.

I used to get high of alcohol but now I am proud to say I get a million times higher than that, I can't get any higher than Jesus Christ and without any side effects ever. From here on out, I have no fear or doubt, He is my Commander.

These days I use Jesus' word He spoke straight out the gospel to fight my personal demons. I find it far more effective than drowning my sorrows and self medicating on copious amounts of alcohol, which only makes matters so much worse. The situations I find myself in are only as bad as my reaction to them. God has given me a new direction on which to follow.

Sober Craig therefore commands the enemy of all evil to surrender to the Cross. The second tree that Jesus bore all our sins with, on the day He was crucified over 2000 years ago. He suffered unimaginable persecution, torture, suffering and torrent abuse and did not deserve any of it, because after all, He never sinned, not once. I remember times when I got the blame for something I never did, I could not stand it. However, He did all that and more, so that we all shall live and I believe God almighty resurrected His body and Jesus arose from the tomb three days later. Thank you Lord, my Redeemer lives.

I believe that particular cross, not only gives life, but eternal life to anyone who believes in it. I consider it is the second tree; the first was the tree of knowledge in the days of Adam and Eve. So with all this in mind, I Craig, resist the enemy, rebuke him, and from my spirit he shall flee.

(James 4:7)
    In the holy name of Jesus Christ, our Lord.
(John 10:10)
    The thief comes only to kill, steal and destroy.
(1 John 4:8) (2 timothy 1:7)
    God is love, power and a sound mind;
(Isaiah 53:5)
    And by His stripes we are (were) healed.

There is power, power, wonder working power every day and every hour, in the precious blood of the Lamb.

The King of majesty is Lord Jesus Christ. I know it's the blood for me. I owe my life to Him.

Personally, I did not have to change; Jesus Christ came into my life and changed me instead. I am so glad I searched for His love and guidance, I am overjoyed with the result, He has blessed me with a wonderful family and true friends, and blissful happiness.

It did not matter whether I believed in Him or not, He believed in me and has done ever since and before my birth and continues to do so. Praise the Lord.

Given time, I will do whatever He wants me to do and become whoever He wants me to be.

Some glad morning when this life is over I'll fly away; and when I die, hallelujah, by and by, I'll fly away. What a wonderful song, it teaches me not to be afraid of death, but to work towards reaching heaven which I am 100 percent positive exists in the after life. On my judgement day I want to make sure, I have done my very best here on earth to enter the pearly gates of heaven. My pastor told our congregation that he believed righteousness was to be able to stand in front of God without fear of condemnation, which is my ultimate goal.

Another thing I am sure of is that on this earth; God hasn't finished with me yet!

Jesus lives . . .

I am living proof there's a God, I truly believe that. I decided to write this testimony about my struggle with the devil and how I fought him through Jesus Christ, our Lord in heaven. I am reflecting on my journey to Christ who is my only gateway to the heavenly Father. Now with Christ in my life for the first real time I can say I am happy. I use Scriptures everyday, speak them by mouth and they fight satan for me.

I have to admit I have had to rewrite this testimony, as I preached too much to other people what they should do to get Christ in their lives. It came across as too aggressive and forceful, I regret my actions and furthermore I am not like that. Plus I feel I am a hypocrite when I do not live the Bible word for word yet, so how on earth can I dare to preach to others what they should do. Fear not though, I have seen the error of my ways and now this book is purely me reminiscing on my life. I have included Scriptures from different versions of the Bible to cross-reference my experiences, I am not preaching to anyone this time; they are simply included to describe how they relate to my life.

Matthew 23:25-26: "Woe to you, teachers of the law and Pharisees, you hypocrites! You clean the outside of the cup and dish, but inside they are full of greed and self-indulgence. You blind Pharisee! First clean the inside of the cup and dish, and then the outside also will be clean."

My eldest brother has inspired me and through his advice I will change this book to my own personal voyage with the Lord God almighty. After my supernatural encounter with Jesus, I am in no doubt that God knows me in detail as an individual, everything I have done, and knows every little strand on my head.

Matthew 10:29-31: "Are not two sparrows sold for a penny? Yet not one of them will fall to the ground apart from the will of your Father. And even the very hairs of your head are all numbered. So don't be afraid; you are worth more than many sparrows."

In my life I have always needed to acquire a good strong faith in God (whose name in my Bible is I am). I have read the Bible once while staying with a lovely Christian couple in Sydney, Australia. I have listened to audio CD's from various pastors who gave me the ultimate advice on how to carry out my life according to the Gospel. Every night we used to discuss a chapter of the good book and then sing some wonderful hymns. It did me wonders then but unfortunately when I got back home to England I morphed back to my usual self, my only first interest was the dreaded drink.

I was diagnosed with Bi Polar Disorder so I know a lot of people will just think I have gone crazy. In fact I was crazy, I fell ill about five years ago and was saying some ridiculous things about religion and at one point, I was so high I actually thought I was God (I am sorry, I repent). Personally, I once believed my Bi Polar Disorder was not a mental health illness but a test from God. Would my life be spent serving satan through a life of sin and be killed spiritually, mentally and physically or worshipping Jesus Christ who gives eternal life to all that accept Him?

Another term for Bi Polar Disorder is Manic Depression; unfortunately some Manic Depressives never get to talk about their lives because they have succeeded in killing themselves. I was protected by Christ to have this wonderful opportunity to share my story.

Every day since I discovered Jesus lives, I have spoken to him. He gives me guidance like typing this now for instance. It is a wonderful experience and it is making me a much better person. In fact one day I would like to become a shining example of maybe how to live. I use the Lord's existence and his teaching in the Gospel as an example of how I should treat and respect others, live my life and above all pray to God. I am finding by reading the Bible again, I am further developing my relationship with the Father of creation.

Matthew 7:12: "So in everything, do to others what you would have them do to you, for this sums up the Law and the Prophets."

The devil comes in many forms whether it's through the media, wars, alcohol, drugs, smoking, gambling, lust or even television. I am getting all this guidance from our Father in heaven who chose the right path for me. God perfectly entered my life in time before I hit thirty; I will never see forty without him.

Jesus Christ heals all, no matter your faith, race, creed, colour, and sex or sexual preference. I even walked away once claiming I was an agnostic, but not now; now I believe every word of the Bible and I worship Jesus Christ; I am proud that He is present in my life. I now know my purpose in life is to serve him all my days and help people believe in him or reignite the believer's existing faith. If my testimony can save one person in this world or help them cut down on their drinking. I will feel I have answered His call and carried out His good works. The Bible states put your trust in the Lord; He has always put his trust in me.

Proverbs 3:5: "Trust in the Lord with all your heart, and lean not on your own understanding; in all your ways acknowledge Him, and He shall direct your paths."

Heavy drinking got me into so much trouble; I realise now it was the father of lies, who worked in my life to try to stop me from finding God. I am not proud of it but I have consumed more alcohol in ten years than the average human being's entire lifetime. I used to be arrogant of drinking twenty pints in a day, now I realise what a fool I was, and a fool with his money are easily parted. I am ashamed to say that through drink I have wet the bed over a hundred times. Not only on my own bed, other people's furniture, and mattresses and once I even defecated myself, all because of the dreaded drug known to the world as alcohol.

It took me until I was twenty-nine to admit I was an alcoholic.

I would always indulge in my fantasy about women who are heavily endowed. I have never had a real relationship in my life, my wife and partner was always alcohol. Alcohol cost me a lot of money. I could never have nice things in the latter stages of my disease as it would be expended on beer, cider or whatever I could lay my hands on.

Money in the wrong hands, I believe, can be the cause of war, poverty, marriage break ups, prostitution, murder and death. I gave all my money to the evil one, he stole from me and destroyed my life; but he never killed me and he just cannot seem to slay me because Jesus Christ is protecting me.

Matthew 6:24: "No one can serve two masters, for either he will hate the one and love the other, or he will be devoted to the one and despise the other. You cannot serve God and money."

I must have spent in the region of one hundred thousand pounds on what I can only describe as poison. However when it came to music and films, I would not spend a penny to watch them. At the cinema you couldn't drink beer and smoke cigarettes while you watch the movie so I didn't go, I just watched them on my computer. One thing I have changed now and I am happy to say so, is I no longer illegally download music or films off the internet any more, I see now I was stealing.

In fact my drinking got so severe I never even had a good time socialising, because I would have up to ten cans before I left the front door. No one would really want to talk to me because I would be foaming at the mouth and not making a word of sense. So I grew wise to it in the end, I would drink in pubs during the day, the earliest of which opened at nine in the morning then eventually retire back to my living room in the afternoon and drink there alone. My only friends I felt I had in that dark place I was in, was the television and my cans of beer. When I woke up, I felt miserable, depressed, upset and I never did remember what I had watched the day before. If only I would have drank from Christ's fountain sooner instead of selling my soul to the devil.

John 4:14: "but whoever drinks the water I give him will never thirst. Indeed, the water I give him will become in him a spring of water welling up to eternal life."

On a positive note I have received good advice from my brothers, fathers, sisters mother, pastors, fire fighters, psychiatrists, councillors, soldiers, paramedics, doctors, nurses and Alcoholics Anonymous. Not to mention all the other great people I have encountered and friends I have met along the way on my journey to Christ. Even though I just have a regular job in a supermarket at the moment, I am already planning what to do with my life once I leave there, and leave for a better existence I will in Israel.

I am truly blessed to have found the author of all life and I'm not crazy any more, He healed me.

I have a different thought pattern and a different perspective now and I don't want to waste all my money I earn on alcoholic drinks, I have to stop smoking as well because that will kill me eventually. Also I realise now by being an alcoholic I was just tithing to pubs, shops and supermarkets, even the Government in VAT charges. All to wake up broke, regretful and feeling like the living dead. I have already stopped viewing pornographic material, further proof my life-changing experience isn't just down to quitting drink.

John 10:10-11: "The thief cometh not, but for to steal, and to kill, and to destroy: I am come that they might have life, and that they might have it more abundantly. I am the good shepherd: the good shepherd giveth his life for the sheep."

These words help me overcome the demons in my life each day, to me, the devil is real and he will tear you apart if you let him. However he is not as strong as Christ, in fact nowhere near as powerful. Everyday I talk to the Lord for guidance; I know He gave his life up so that I could live. There is wonderful power in the blood of the Lamb.

John 3:16: "For God so loved the world that he gave his one and only Son, that whoever believes in him shall not perish but have eternal life."

I have decided I want to go somewhere more peaceful, anywhere in the world to relax and let my spiritual side grow and be nurtured. I'll find a job because I'm not inebriated any more. You work to live, not the opposite way around.

Giant corporations are consumed by greed and have a different cutthroat point of view than mine. You know what though; those huge bosses may be millionaires or even billionaires and even though I have no money, in fact I'm penniless, I am happy.

Nonetheless I have the greatest prosperity of all in my soul—Jesus Christ.

Once I stopped serving money as my master, I have a completely different outlook on life. As far as I'm concerned Christ and His love makes the world go around not money, He lives and will soon return to put the world right again.

A lady at an A.A meeting once shared to me that the only thing I have to change is everything. Indeed changing everything more or less in me will take time, but is obtainable with some hard toil. I mean do not get me wrong, I do want some money, a house and a family of my own some day, but I have come to realise that the best things in life are free. God's love for me was free after all and always has been.

Mathew 19:24: "Again I tell you, it is easier for a camel to go through the eye of a needle than for a rich man to enter the kingdom of God."

Alcohol was very expensive for me when I almost lost everything through it. I even used to sell all my prized possessions like amplifiers, guitar pedals and computer games to get hold of some. However money isn't my master anymore, neither is satan, It's all up to me now to stop the devil coming back into my life and that of my family. In fact it took me a lifetime to realise I had to change my ways. I didn't work hard enough, I smelled, I was always drunk or hung-over, the thief took a stranglehold of my life. With one touch from Jesus Christ, everything changed in me for the better.

I turn my thoughts to the Old Testament.

Job was a righteous man and did not have the luxury of Christ to follow in his life, but his faith in God was so strong he made it through all his hardships, afflictions and suffering anyway.

Job 13:15: "Though he slay me, yet will I trust in him"

I have the opportunity to have his kind of faith and follow Jesus Christ. If I achieve that; the world would be fond of me rather than reject me. Job went through torture and misery but was rewarded after his battle with the dark lord by our merciful Father in heaven. Another good example of this test of faith is sAbraham, who was willing to kill his own son Isaac to prove his almighty faith in God.

Genesis 22:1-19: "Then God said, 'Take your son, your only son, whom you love—Isaac—and go to the region of Moriah. Sacrifice him there as a burnt offering on a mountain I will show you.'"

He proved just how far he was willing to demonstrate his love for our heavenly Father and God responded:

v 12 "Do not lay a hand on the boy," he said. "Do not do anything to him. Now I know that you fear God, because you have not withheld from me your son, your only son."

Personally my battle was with drink. I had to prove to God that I had enough of all the drama, heartache and fear it had brought me and my family. A year ago I was baptised in the sea at one of Sydney's many beautiful beaches and I accepted Him as my Lord and Saviour. I didn't do that alone, the Messiah was there to guide me every step of the way. I had two bottles of wine just before because I didn't know if it would instantly stop me drinking or not. In fact the amount of booze I have had has made me ponder if I deserved it or not, but it didn't seem to matter, He carried me anyway. Exactly one year after the date of my baptism my desire for drink vanished, praise Jesus Christ.

𝕴𝖘𝖆𝖎𝖆𝖍 46:3-4: "𝕷𝖎𝖘𝖙𝖊𝖓 𝖙𝖔 𝖒𝖊, ⊘ 𝖍𝖔𝖚𝖘𝖊 𝖔𝖋 𝕵𝖆𝖈𝖔𝖇, 𝖆𝖑𝖑 𝖞𝖔𝖚 𝖜𝖍𝖔 𝖗𝖊𝖒𝖆𝖎𝖓 𝖔𝖋 𝖙𝖍𝖊 𝖍𝖔𝖚𝖘𝖊 𝖔𝖋 𝕴𝖘𝖗𝖆𝖊𝖑, 𝖞𝖔𝖚 𝖜𝖍𝖔𝖒 𝕴 𝖍𝖆𝖛𝖊 𝖚𝖕𝖍𝖊𝖑𝖉 𝖘𝖎𝖓𝖈𝖊 𝖞𝖔𝖚 𝖜𝖊𝖗𝖊 𝖈𝖔𝖓𝖈𝖊𝖎𝖛𝖊𝖉, 𝖆𝖓𝖉 𝖍𝖆𝖛𝖊 𝖈𝖆𝖗𝖗𝖎𝖊𝖉 𝖘𝖎𝖓𝖈𝖊 𝖞𝖔𝖚𝖗 𝖇𝖎𝖗𝖙𝖍.

Even to your old age and grey hairs I am he, I am he who will sustain you. I have made you and I will carry you; I will sustain you and I will rescue you."

He carried me through alcoholism and for that alone I am eternally grateful to God. Alcohol plays a part in everyone's life whether they drink or not. It is plentiful in society, crime, love, hate and violence. All your emotions are magnified ten times over whether you're happy, sad or even angry. If Christ hadn't saved me from my sinful drinking, I would either be homeless, imprisoned or find myself in a mental asylum or worse dead.

I almost drank myself to death and have received not one but several miracles.

I tried to kill myself in the fire service by jumping thirty two feet, that didn't kill me. Another suicide attempt with one hundred pills, that didn't kill me, neither did up to twenty-four cans of strong beer in one night. My binge drinking made me so unbelievably paranoid, I couldn't stand being in crowds of people because of the fifty can, three day bender I'd been on. I recall horrible feelings travelling on the bus and when I got to work and I saw an army of customers, a hundred or so, I had a nervous breakdown. I played the Bi Polar card and booked sick, I had to and it took me seven pints just to feel normal.

All I could cope with was being isolated, watching the TV, drinking and smoking.

I realise now I wasn't just paying to kill myself, I was in my mind heading straight to hell, that's how bad it felt.

𝕬𝖈𝖙𝖘 2:29-31: " . . . 𝖑𝖊𝖙 𝖒𝖊 𝖋𝖗𝖊𝖊𝖑𝖞 𝖘𝖕𝖊𝖆𝖐 𝖚𝖓𝖙𝖔 𝖞𝖔𝖚 𝖔𝖋 𝖙𝖍𝖊 𝖕𝖆𝖙𝖗𝖎𝖆𝖗𝖈𝖍 𝕯𝖆𝖛𝖎𝖉, 𝖙𝖍𝖆𝖙 𝖍𝖊 𝖎𝖘 𝖇𝖔𝖙𝖍 𝖉𝖊𝖆𝖉 𝖆𝖓𝖉 𝖇𝖚𝖗𝖎𝖊𝖉 . . . 𝕿𝖍𝖊𝖗𝖊𝖋𝖔𝖗𝖊 𝖇𝖊𝖎𝖓𝖌 𝖆 𝖕𝖗𝖔𝖕𝖍𝖊𝖙, 𝖆𝖓𝖉 𝖐𝖓𝖔𝖜𝖎𝖓𝖌 𝖙𝖍𝖆𝖙 𝕲𝖔𝖉 𝖍𝖆𝖉 𝖘𝖜𝖔𝖗𝖓 𝖜𝖎𝖙𝖍 𝖆𝖓 𝖔𝖆𝖙𝖍 𝖙𝖔 𝖍𝖎𝖒, 𝖙𝖍𝖆𝖙 𝖔𝖋 𝖙𝖍𝖊 𝖋𝖗𝖚𝖎𝖙 𝖔𝖋 𝖍𝖎𝖘 𝖑𝖔𝖎𝖓𝖘, 𝖆𝖈𝖈𝖔𝖗𝖉𝖎𝖓𝖌 𝖙𝖔 𝖙𝖍𝖊 𝖋𝖑𝖊𝖘𝖍, 𝖍𝖊 𝖜𝖔𝖚𝖑𝖉 𝖗𝖆𝖎𝖘𝖊 𝖚𝖕 𝕮𝖍𝖗𝖎𝖘𝖙 𝖙𝖔 𝖘𝖎𝖙 𝖔𝖓 𝖍𝖎𝖘 𝖙𝖍𝖗𝖔𝖓𝖊; 𝕳𝖊 seeing this before spake of the resurrection of Christ, that his soul was not left in hell, neither his flesh did see corruption."

I have chosen the road to heaven wisely, I can be whatever I want to be, confident, successful and happy or just a hopeless alcoholic drunk, well that was me before Christ anyway, many people can testify to that. He came into my life on the 27th of February 2010, A few days later, His force was so strong that I crashed to my knees and I confessed my love to Him. A love that is stronger than that, I give to my parents. I also now recognize the fact, that what I lack in Biblical knowledge; God has compensated for with the Lord's blessing which has restored normality to me. I have received love, power, strength and knowledge beyond my wildest dreams because God gave me the mind of Christ.

1 Corinthians 2:14-1: "The unspiritual man does not receive the gifts of the Spirit of God, for they are folly to him, and he is not able to understand them because they are spiritually discerned. The spiritual man judges all things, but is himself to be judged by no one. For who has known the mind of the Lord so as to instruct Him? But we have the mind of Christ."

I recognise that my experience of pain is nowhere near as much as what Jesus suffered over 2000 years ago. He bore our sins on the cross that day and went through unimaginable torture. The Lord made the ultimate sacrifice for the good of the world and mankind. I consider sometimes what I can offer in return.

Matthew 16:24: "Then Jesus said to his disciples, If anyone would come after me, he must deny himself and take up his cross and follow me. For whoever wants to save his life will lose it, but whoever loses his life for me will find it. What good will it be for a man if he gains the whole world, yet forfeits his soul? Or what can a man give in exchange for his soul?"

I believe the thief jumped into my life March 15th 2000, when the Sergeant Major came to our house and told us that my brother had died from gunshot wounds to his head from an automatic rifle. He fled my soul 11 years later when my Dad died. I believe my Dad went to heaven, spoke to Jesus and said "can you sort Craig out please for goodness sake". My mind has experienced in the last few weeks peace and serenity and I'm overjoyed with myself.

2 Timothy 1:7: "For God hath not given us the spirit of fear; but of power, and of love, and of a sound mind."

This is another powerful Scripture I am trying hard to digest in my mind. I am replacing alcohol with the Word of God and it doesn't cost a penny to read the Bible. I'm not even telling people not to drink, I want everyone to enjoy their lives. If you're a sensible drinker, you deserve a drink to relax with after work but not me; I can't stop once I have started. One is too much and ten are not enough any more, so I wave goodbye to it. I want to turn tragedy into triumph with a little help from you know who. In fact Christ has helped me enough though; I have to repay the favour by being kind to others and think of them rather than just myself from now on. In doing so, I will have a more abundant and meaningful life.

John 15:12: "This is my commandment: love one another as I have loved you."

I truly believe this is my purpose in life to tell people there is a God and share my story. An evangelist in Sydney, Australia once preached to me, that the good things you do in your life isn't just down to you, it is the works of Christ. I never believed it back then, but now I am certain when he spoke that day he had; and still has; the mind of Christ. I think everyone in the world fights satan from the day they are born; he attacks your physical strength, your mental capacity, health, soul, Spirit and eventually your life.

Jeremiah 29:11: "For I know the thoughts that I think toward you, says the Lord, thoughts of peace and not of evil, to give you a future and a hope."

I bet he planted the idea of how to make alcohol into someone's head to cause the chaos in the world, then, now, and in the future. I would never have believed when I was younger, that I could communicate with God; I really can though now,

I mean it from the bottom of my heart, these words are not my own but of Christ.

I have never had so much interest in anything than reading the Bible, writing, typing and thinking of God. This compared to serving the devil, becoming paralytic every night angry, sad, depressed and lonely, all through booze.

Matthew Chapter 8:1-3: "When He (Jesus) had come down from the mountain, great multitudes followed Him. And behold, a leper came and worshipped Him, saying,

'Lord, if you are willing, you can make me clean.' Then Jesus put out His hand and touched him, saying, 'I am willing; be cleansed.' Immediately his leprosy was cleansed".

I wear my silver cross outside of my clothes now because I am proud to show the world that I believe in Jesus Christ. Satan was my sickness, believing in Jesus Christ was the answer and the cure. Jesus heals all sickness and disease. One thing I know for sure he healed me!

Romans 1:16: "For I am not ashamed of the gospel of Christ: for it is the power of God unto salvation to every one that believeth;"

My history of alcohol

Before I continue to discuss my negative experiences, I will begin on a positive note. I have finished my twelve steps of Alcoholics Anonymous today with my sponsor at his house. That is something to be proud of in my eyes considering I almost drank myself to death three weeks ago. All thanks to Jesus Christ again.

They say smoking stunts your growth and it probably does but alcohol definitely stunts your spiritual growth.

Alcohol takes no prisoners and it is relentless, tenacious and unforgiving. It robbed and deprived me of my career, social life, University degree and some of my friends. I am not physically a fighter, neither am I aggressive, but fuelled by alcohol I became precisely both. Here are a few occasions I can remember:

After about fifteen pints one night, I grabbed a man by the throat for no apparent reason. He was an old friend of my deceased brother, about six foot eight and I suspect he was into hard drugs. He could have killed me that night;

I recall I was severely frightened a week or so later when he confronted me in the streets. I said instantly I was sincerely sorry, he then told me the only reason he didn't put me in hospital that night was because of his friendship with my brother.

I was suffering with a raging hangover one day; I had some money so I foolishly returned to the same pub where that incident occurred because the drinks were so cheap. Even though the lager and cider were watered down, I didn't care, I was that unwell I decided to go top shelf as well and got completely hammered. I was in double figures on beer and vodka or brandy, fundamentally anything with lots of alcohol.

Don't get me wrong it starts out as a high for me, but then it turns into a living nightmare where just about anything could go wrong. For a start I don't know how I got home but I did manage to somehow, I then stupidly tripped over on a low railing and couldn't get up or even walk without help. Luckily enough my next door neighbour picked me up and took me to my front door, I know the Lord sent him to help me, I thank Jesus and my neighbour.

Matthew 19:19: "Honour thy father and thy mother: and, Thou shalt love thy neighbour as thyself."

I left myself so vulnerable and there are people in this world that will take advantage of that fact.

Once again the next morning I think I wet the bed and felt an even almightier hangover where I got the shakes, was incredibly paranoid, depressed, anxious and above all I was left feeling hopeless.

I can't believe it took me this long to stop it. My whole world revolved around alcohol. I was definitely dependent on it to self medicate and control my moods, whether I was high or low. That alone should have stopped me drinking but I never did. Other side effects of my heavy drinking were that it made me very loud, hyper, inconsiderate and obnoxious. I was fooling around in the early hours of the morning outside a major train station. I conversed with this stranger's girlfriend and kicked a bottle right at his head without realising.

He did take a loud comment I made out of context, but it didn't matter, he still head butted me right on the bridge of my nose and it bled. My so called friends I had met that night soon scarpered and I felt awful with myself. Strangely enough though, it was the best thing that could have possibly happened to me. A bouncer in a night club said he could have me killed for saying something offensive a few hours before this incident. This one night experience did not stop me drinking but it calmed me down a bit and I stopped wandering the streets of a major city at stupid o' clock in the morning.

I first almost met my Maker about eight years ago, I was sick after a watch night out, I remained in the pub after everyone had decided to go, and it was a bad idea. My drink was spiked with perhaps GHB (liquid ecstasy) and my colleague who is an attractive female had it happen to her. I don't even remember leaving the bar; I would not be surprised if the bouncers escorted me from the premises.

Once outside I had already been picked up by police and taken to a taxi rank.

The taxi driver must have kicked me out, I don't know. I ended up in this field and had an out of body experience. It was crazy man, I could see myself from behind and I had no control, it must have been the devil's influence because I smashed some windows and broke into a residential home. I looked around and there were two police officers ready to handcuff me, arrest me and stick me in the back of a police van. It turned out they were the same officers that had previously dropped me off at the taxi rank.

I remember a horrible lonely feeling as the cell door shut for the night. The next morning I was interviewed and asked to come back in a week's time for a caution. Because I was in the emergency services, I was told I had to tell my boss. We had a new Station Officer, a bit like a Sergeant Major in the Army, my old boss would have understood but not this one. I was so scared, confused and concerned I would lose my job, I planned my own death.

The police dropped me off about five miles from home to catch a bus but I decided to walk home instead. I was that depressed and miserable I looked to the sky and said I'll be joining you (my brother) up there in heaven. When I returned home, my eldest and compassionate brother took one look at me and he advised me not to go to work, but I asked my best mate to give me a lift anyway.

First I tried to enter a high rise tower block but could not get into the premises as the entrance was sealed and secured for demolition. I went back to the Fire Station I served at, I avoided anyone there and sneaked into the office and grabbed the keys for the training tower. I remember fear as I had never felt it before as I walked up those steps. I got to the third floor and decided this was high enough, this would do the job, the next was the highest floor and I was too scared to climb those steps. The windows had no glass, just a big open sill.

I straddled my legs either side of the sill and threw myself off it from thirty-
two feet onto solid concrete. It was so high I was frightened and I changed my mind in mid-air, I no longer wanted to die, and blacked out.

I woke up in a critical care ward four days later; the first people I saw was my Mum and Dad, I was so glad to see them both. Jesus Christ saved me then and I didn't realise it. I was bruised and battered and I think stayed in hospital for ten weeks. They wouldn't give me any more morphine either because I got hooked on that too. I came out in a wheelchair but I felt so lucky and happy to be alive I didn't get down about it. Quite the opposite. I planned a trip to Disney World, Orlando, Florida to help me to recover.

Another crazy event happened in the Fire Service, It may have been the work of God. I was getting mistreated so badly by a high ranking officer. I mean don't get me wrong, I had it coming for being badly behaved and going A.W.O.L but I didn't deserve the level of harassment I got. We rarely get tornados in England, but one came out of nowhere, demolished her roof and other houses, yet I consider no one was hurt, Praise the Lord, if indeed it was Him.

I got unfairly dismissed in the end; consequently I started self-medicating on obscene amounts of alcohol. A few months later I was so sick and depressed about losing my fantastic career; I downed one hundred tablets and washed them down with eight cans of beer so I would not wake up. I had no thought or consideration for my Mum who would have discovered her other son dead, for that I am really sorry. However it never killed me because of Christ's intervention yet again. As soon as I woke up I ran into the bathroom and threw up in the sink. I didn't tell anyone for days, so there was nothing the hospital could do for me. I suffered severe muscle cramps for days, but after that my liver regenerated and I survived, Praise the Lord once more. I now realise just how precious life is, but it's a relief to know I am under his angelic wing.

I have done so many things I am ashamed of in England never mind the rest of the world. Using my student loan to finance my drinking, I visited my eldest brother to a have a laugh with him and have a lot of beer of course. I had roughly seven pints and then got another eight cans at least. My elder sister came around for a bit with her three kids, I had recently swopped a game with her only son, and I did not like the game so I told him to his face. I resent the fact that I had been vicious towards him. I spoke to him aggressively and nastily, I am again mortified by my conduct in my past.

I went around the next day, and all I was concerned about was getting three pounds off my father for some cans of beer, My Dad (r.i.p) wanted me to stay and drink pop instead, but I was so paranoid and miserable that I just wanted the money (not stay with my loving family) and I then retired back to my house to, you guessed it—sit in front of the T.V again with only four cans of lager this time.

A few days later my brother had a talk with me and I sincerely apologised to my sister and her son, I am lucky she forgave me, it was another lesson in how boozing transformed everything about me.

Another time, I was in a popular and inexpensive pub one day and I was on a high, and I did not realise the consequences of my words. I spotted my Aunty, who I have great respect for now; because of all the support she gave my Mum after my brother had committed suicide in the Army. I am ashamed to share the fact that I proclaimed I had done the best out of my entire family. I deeply regret those words and I still need to apologise to my uncle who is a strong family man, who took my words to heart.

Like satan himself, alcohol was cunning, deceitful, manipulative and deadly to me. It stole my true identity and character and killed my morals.

I believe that it is apparent that God has swooped down from heaven and said to Himself, I will have him from now on; I am definitely part of his divine plan. When I first visited that healing church in Sydney, the evangelist understood that I had a different energy surrounding me, I believe him now. But I digress, the best of all is, that it is not like a regular job serving the Lord, I feel as though I can not do enough for him, in return for his blessing.

I am beyond doubt that is if I remain true to the Gospel, live Jesus'

Commandments and not give in to the thief's temptation on earth, the kingdom of God can be mine. I sense satan's grip on me loosening everyday as I serve God, and get to know Christ more and more. I recall another event where I again tried to commit suicide by jumping off a high reservoir. This time however the Lord miraculously changed my mind and I turned around and journeyed home, praise Jesus.

The next time the Lord stepped into my life to protect me was the last time I had a drink. Heavy binge drinking again, I was in no fit state to go to work.

Every incident was exacerbated because I could not function without a drink. I was so stressed that I had a nervous breakdown, booked sick and left the store.

I had my drinks in the pub to help me get calmer, it didn't work and I was too paranoid to stay. For the next five days I just drank and drank and smoked and watched TV. It was all I knew and could do at the time. Binge drinking transformed me into a compulsive liar, thieving, selfish and slothful man. But when I had that last drink and decided I just didn't want it anymore, all changed for the better, praise Jesus.

I asked my Mum to help me go to AA (Rehab) and after a few meetings I felt at peace with myself. Next came beautiful serenity, within days after that, Jesus manifested His glory to me and when I realised who it was I crashed to my knees in awe of His presence. Then I started to get this lovely feeling in my stomach, and then a week after that, I feel that I was given the Holy Spirit and the mind of Christ, Praise the Lord over and over again.

I would recommend to anyone with a dark past or a problem with drink or drugs to give Jesus Christ a try in your life. It will be the best thing you have ever done, believe me and what have you got to lose?

One thing about the Son of Man I am surprised about is that that He has a jovial, comical side to Him. He gets me typing things that I cannot help but express amusement at. His sense of humour is epic. Take all the good attributes of everyone on Earth and roll them into one and you get Christ.

If everyone on earth knew how wonderful it felt to start living a holy lifestyle, attempt to cut out sin/the thief from their lives and followed the Gospel's command, then I believe the world would be saved until Christ's return.

I know I should get back to the basics of loving and learning from all the people I encounter, give praise for the food I eat and enjoy God's creation for what it is.

I am not positive, but it seems to me that anyone who is Bi Polar can communicate with God, I can. We are in the last book of the Bible still, the book of Revelation; my testimony is part of God's almighty plan.

Bi Polar humans are more susceptible to the thief's wicked ways. They have a major problem with addiction right across the board. The extreme mood experiences they suffer could be a spiritual battle in their brain between choosing good or bad in their life. When they are down, they are depressed and near suicidal. When they are up and high, they go off like a bottle of pop. A lot of Bi Polar people commit suicide sadly because the thief has sickened their minds with a horrible, uncontrollable sense of fear. I am one of the lucky ones to survive all my suicide attempts thanks again to our Redeemer, Saviour and Lord Jesus Christ.

I once read on a sign outside a gym in Sydney that a healthy mind starts with a fit body, I am a rapidly recovering alcoholic with Christ at my side and will live those words for the benefit of me, my family and my friends.

My life is far more fulfilling with Jesus Christ in my life than alcohol (the thief) could ever offer me. In fact, I have determined that my consumption of alcohol for a period of around twelve years was just another chapter in my bizarre but interesting life.

Even though these words are not biblical, the serenity prayer spoken at the end of every Alcoholic Anonymous meeting speaks wonders to everyone who shares at the meetings.

O God and Heavenly Father,

Grant to us the serenity of mind to accept that which cannot be changed; courage to change that which can be changed, and wisdom to know the one from the other, through Jesus Christ our Lord, Amen.

Only a few months ago, my mate took me out delivering some stock in the capital for the day. He was sober because he was driving, needless to say that I was not. I enjoyed my first eight cans of strong cider and I had a great laugh with him on the way to London. We drove past the fantastic sights that the capital had to offer. I saw the 02 arena, the Olympic village/ stadium, millionaire's row and the skyscrapers of the financial quarter.

However it was a different story on the return journey, I bought another six cans of strong lager and the rest was history. I must have blacked out in the van, left the front door to my house wide open and crashed out on my bed in my room. My Mum had returned from an Alcoholic's Anonymous meeting only to think we had been burgled. We had an almighty argument the following morning, so I got out of the way to nurse my hangover. I hid in pubs in the town and spent the remainder of the money that I had earned all on booze. I planned to have two hours sleep before work whilst my mum had returned to finish the rest of her day at work. I could have got the sack for being drunk and having beer cans in my bag but I never, I must have hid it well. When I used to drink a lot, I must have resembled the devil in some respect, because I got very good at the art of lying.

I recall I visited my dear old friend who was having her birthday party. I was looking better physically and it started out great for me but I soon deteriorated. I had drunk my eight cans of strong lager within two hours, and then stole three more from the fridge on top of half the free punch available. I was foaming at the mouth apparently and not making a word of sense. In the end her husband paid for a taxi to take me home,

I regret that maybe it was to get rid of me but I am still thankful. I woke up in the morning with a raging hangover and I had wet the bed again. I picked up my bag in the morning and it felt really heavy. There were two take away curries and half a bottle of red wine. It all came flooding back to me that I was that scared when they had ordered me a taxi of not having any booze to go home to.

That I just took/stole the bottle and I was alarmed to later know that my actions as a consequence may have caused a fight afterwards. I am really sorry to her for committing those iniquities; but I also realise it was all because of the dreaded drink we call alcohol. I also apologise to the possible person who could have been accused that night of doing what they thought I would not do, my alcoholism was so advanced then that it came first and everything else came a distant second.

Holidays were both fun and traumatic

In my life I have been blessed and privileged to have seen a fair bit of the world which God created.

My Dad, Mum and I took a vacation in Ayia Napa, Cyprus, so that we could visit the United Nations post in Nicosia where my brother tragically died. On the way home on the coach, a stranger befriended me and I confided in him. I later found out from my eldest brother that he was a reporter and he had my story printed in the local paper back home. I trusted him, and he lied and manipulated me in to giving him a story that ultimately sells papers for you guessed it, money. This happened even though my Mum and Dad had asked the Sergeant Major to respect our privacy and let us grieve in peace.

I went skiing in Andorra with Green Watch from my Fire Station. I got so badly burnt from being on the slopes the previous day. I recall my face was unrecognisable, bruised and battered and swollen. My female colleagues who I later refer to in this testimony said if it was going to happen to anyone, it was going to happen to me, I agree. I came out of the hospital with bandages wrapped around my entire face. I swear I looked like an ancient Mummy, and I wore my shades as well and everyone in the streets stared at me and probably had a chuckle. I can see the funny side of it now, but unfortunately I was drinking alone in my room early in the morning whilst everyone else was enjoying skiing on one of a number of God's creations which he made in six days.

Orlando, Florida, is an amazing place with so much to see and do. I met this wonderful attractive girl but I have to admit she was slowing me down; I wanted to see everything there. She invited me back about six months later to stay with her in her apartment for two weeks. By this time though my drinking had escalated, I got jealous of whoever was going to have her instead of me. She told me that she could not figure out if I was this really sweet guy or just a jerk, alcohol and the thief strike again.

In Cancun I felt I was in paradise, turquoise sea, beautiful white sandy beaches and red hot sun. The only trouble was that the hotels were all inclusive. However I hardly ate, I was more concerned with the free bars which were like a red rag to a bull to me.

I moved hotel mainly because the beer was horrible and it was outside the main area where everything happened. At my new hotel I felt better, and met some great mates from Manchester, England. Even they said I am not a bad looking lad and need to calm down with my boozing. Midway through my holiday I took their advice, and slowed down my alcohol consumption.

I decided to go to this aquarium where I was enclosed in a tank and submerged into water containing plenty of sharks. I got to feed a Cat Shark and still have a picture of me amongst Bull Sharks and I loved the Dolphins. I was mesmerised by these God given creatures.

I soon met a wonderful Canadian girl, the best most beautiful lady I have ever had the honour of meeting so far. In fact I told her that she was more beautiful inside and out than these seven other superficial and spoilt American girls (you know the types?) Just walking along the beach at night with her, hand in hand is one of the best memories of my life. She left two days later and I went on another bender on both cocaine and alcohol.

I got so drunk on beer and tequila that I dived into a shallow pool (3 ft high) and split my nose open. A member of staff brought a wheel chair but I did not want to sit down, I realise now that I was experiencing mania (losing my mind).

I can see why they call Las Vegas the city of sin, it really is and I got sucked into its vortex of temptations. I had arguments with security, hotel residents and I spent most of my time at the bar wearing the same pair of yellow shorts I had on all week. I rode the highest rollercoaster in the world 1000 ft in the sky. I felt on top of the world at that stage.

A family enjoyed talking to me at dinner because of my British accent, but I made some rude obscene comments and they rejected my company from then on, all because I was manic and I drank too much alcohol.

My dear old school friend I have known since I was very young was the main reason I was there, she couldn't go, so I thought what the heck I'll go for her.

I met her American female friend, and I really liked her, she was both different and interesting to me. I hope and pray one day she will no longer be an atheist.

She drove me, her Mum and her sister to San Francisco, this was more my kind of town. I got to see the Golden Gate Bridge and visited Alcatraz prison.

However, I spoilt the experience with alcohol once again. She said if you keep drinking you will get fat. She also was the first girl to tell me I was dependent on alcohol to sleep, so I was an alcoholic, I should have listened then but of course I never did.

New York City—I first experienced vivid mania over here, I used to get so high that when I would come down, I just fell asleep in the streets wherever I was standing and once outside the UN headquarters. I was only sober when I was completely broke. One night I found myself walking through Central Park enjoying the free entertainment and ended up talking to these two attractive girls, both were different in shape and ethnicity. I asked for a cigarette but in the back of my mind, I knew they would like my British accent. They stripped naked because they were extremely drunk and pounced on me.

They asked me if I had ever been sexually assaulted before and I responded no, so they had their wicked way with me. Back then I thought this was like every man's dream but not now. Even when I was ill, I hated and still do despise that sinful act the other way round though, please don't get me mistaken.

It all went disastrously wrong as well; because they had lost their bags and one of the girls became hysterical because she didn't have her car keys. Even though she was completely naked beneath and had only a towel to keep her decent.

She didn't care; she just stepped out of Central Park and into the busy mean streets of Manhattan. All because she thought her bag had been stolen and she had been binge drinking, I became aware of an empty one litre bottle of whisky discarded on the grass. I mean for goodness sake; I only wanted a cigarette off one of them and a maybe a bit of female attention. I had passionate sex with the other girl; she told me that she didn't care about her stolen valuables and expensive jewellery, she was really happy to have met me.

After that we became aware of someone sneaking around in the bushes, so I phoned the police and reported it. The cops took us onto the streets and interviewed us. The police separated us when they suspected I had done some indecent act with the girl that strolled around half naked around New York intoxicated. They arrested me there and then, but did not handcuff me and then put me in the back of the cop car and took me to the police station.

I have never harmed a woman in my life, NYPD were going to throw me in jail, but the other mystery girl who claimed her father was in the mafia, and was in a separate room, corroborated my story that I had consensual sex with her.

Incidentally the police found the missing bag, they were that wasted, they forgot they left it about fifteen yards away from where I first noticed them.

I regularly visited Central Park for its supply of water fountains to quench my thirst and survive. Unless I had money, then of course I would be drinking beer instead. I have to admit I manipulated my friends and family to get money, only to blow it on drugs, alcohol and strippers.

I sincerely apologise to all those I affected. I even ran up twelve hundred dollars in reverse charges back to the UK from the payphones. I admit that I scammed roughly five thousand dollars out of them, I still have not paid them back, I am lucky to have friends and family like that as well, who wanted to help me and I simply threw it back in their face, I repent of all those sins.

I became such a compulsive liar and presently realise that I do not deserve any trust back of my friends until I can prove I have changed and pay them back in full.

I could not get served any alcohol in bars because after my passport was stolen, I had no identity to prove I was over twenty one, so I got my hands on hard drugs instead. One particular dealer said it was coke, but when he handed it to me with a plastic pipe, I knew exactly what it was, but I had paid for it already so I had it, that's how I justified it to myself anyway.

I got high on crack cocaine looking over at the Statue of Liberty, I felt great for about a minute but I came down after that and craved more. There were police patrolling the streets everywhere, I was scared of getting caught and ending up in Brooklyn prison which I could also see in the horizon. Those jails in America are horrific institutions to say the least and I would not last long in one of those prisons.

The first time I had crack cocaine was when I was wired thirteen hundred dollars from my friends in the Fire Service. I was on a high and couldn't trust myself with money. I gave it to this barmaid to look after it for me. What a stupid thing to do, a man who had a drink with me the previous night in the same bar, said "do not trust anyone in New York especially her". I ended up doing the opposite. I then ruined the night furthermore smoking crack cocaine and hiding in alleyways so as not to get caught by the feds.

I woke up shocked to find out I had about only three hundred dollars left, eventually I realised there was four two hundred dollar notes missing. I returned to the bar manic after that, I recall that I pretended I was a police man because I had my Fire Brigade sweater on. I called the police, but they couldn't do anything without proof. I chased the bar manager down the streets into another bar but couldn't find him. I screamed in the pub, are all American people stupid and could have got brutally harmed from bigger men than me. I have nothing against Americans, in fact I like them; I was just confused and extremely sick.

I was only supposed to be in New York City for four days, I was there for four weeks in the end. I came home in only shorts and t shirt, trainers, an empty wallet, maxed out bank cards, temporary passport and a dead phone.

Belfast—I wanted to see where my deceased grandmother came from, Cork I think.

However I couldn't afford to go to the republic of Ireland so I got a one way ticket to Belfast instead, I did not intend on returning. At first I never got out the airport, I drank up to 20 pints mixed with some of my new friend's Polish vodka. The security was absolutely crazy because of the failed liquid bomb terror attacks. I got in big trouble with their police and was questioned intensively, but in the end they called an ambulance and I went to hospital, they even gave me about three pounds to help me survive.

The psychiatrist there recognized I needed medication to stabilise my mood swings. I walked back about ten miles back to the airport, it rained torrentially and it was a real eye opener to see all the Union Jack flags and the kerbs/lampposts were painted in red, white and blue. My best friend, who helped me out with money in New York, helped me again to get home. Even the female fire-fighters told me I was irresponsible on the phone, but were still willing to help me get home, they are all true friends.

City of Sydney—Whilst everyone else was planning their journey backpacking around Australia, I was nursing my hangover in a certain betting bar most days that opened at eight in the morning. It appeared to me that I was the only one drinking alcohol. I never spent a penny on the slot machines; mainly because I never wanted to lose my drinking money.

About ten schooners later, I went to the store to buy more beer. I then retired back to this huge busy hostel which had a pool bar, well that was what me and my new friend who was ex RAF called it. I used to drink, look at the planes fly over the city's horizon and go to sleep in the day, wake up and drink again. I got stuck in this vicious circle and spent near enough two thousand pounds in a matter of weeks.

I am still thankful to my friend for getting us out of one of the most expensive cities in the world. The girl from London I will refer to later about worked at this hostel in a beach resort as a cleaner. We instantly had a friendly face to recognise, I liked most people there and the two managers that run the place were great too and they found me work. Things were going to be ok or so I thought. One lovely thing happened though that occurred in that City centre, another girl from London texted me saying I was officially the sweetest guy she had ever met.

On New Years Eve in Sydney, Australia I was over excited to say the least looking forward to seeing the awesome firework display at midnight. I went for a breakfast where my friend from London was working as a waitress. I told her I would wait until she finished work and accompany her to Sydney Harbour Bridge and the Opera house. Everyone else was going there early, I thought I was doing a good deed but it all went horribly wrong.

I got a twenty four pack of beer at nine in the morning, sat in the manager's office with him while he was sorting out his bills. I just drunk can after can and watched music television.

I then secretly took an ecstasy tablet that was intended for the night time. I went out the office, probably for a cigarette and returned horrified to notice the door locked, the rest of my beer was in the fridge. Never fear though, I forgot I had given eight beers to another mate in the hostel, so he was honest enough to give them back.

I blacked out, apparently my friend who finished work and took me to the train station said I was worried about not having my phone on me, so I walked back onto the platform, returned to the hostel and must have collapsed onto my bed. I woke up at fifteen minutes before midnight to an apparently empty hostel.

Except there was one old gentleman, he was in the television lounge, he swore at me terribly when I asked to watch the celebrations on TV. That was another attempt from the thief to break my spirit and soul; in fact he had been at work inside me all day long . . .

I still had about ten cans left in my bag though, so I sat outside smoking, drinking, a bit depressed and lonely, but relieved I had plenty of beer. My brother, Dad and Mum spoke to me on the phone that I thought I had lost, at midnight to wish me happy New Year. They were probably relieved to know I was safe at least. A young Frenchman talked with me that night and we had a good time conversing with each other. Two months later, he was kicked out the hostel for his unacceptable behaviour and heavy drinking.

I woke up the next day shaking and sad listening to everyone saying how amazing their New Year experience was. I started drinking and the manager spotted me throwing up so he kicked me out. I broke down in tears; I had hardly any money and nowhere to go. He compromised with me that I could stay but only if I had no alcohol; because he would eject me from the premises if I did and I do not blame him. I was just very grateful for the olive branch he gave me and started smoking weed outside the hostel instead. At least that stuff grows from the ground and was made from God, not by man and the thief, like alcohol is.

After a time I got jealous with everyone else's partying, because it was both a working and a wild, fun merrymaking hostel with an awesome but drunken atmosphere. I had plenty of friends but two particular girls, an Estonian girl and a girl from the U.K'S Capital I trusted the most.

Eventually I decided to start drinking by the beach. The trouble with this was that if I got caught by the police, I would have been awarded a four hundred dollar, on the spot fine.

I recall an incident where I and another friend, who was also Bi Polar, had been drinking on the train on our way back from work in the City. He got caught on the train station platform and was fined 800 dollars all together; my bottle was in my pocket so the plain clothed officers were not suspicious of me, Thank the Lord.

But again I digress, one day whilst drinking by the beach; I overheard a man preaching about God. I thought he was crazy (how wrong I was). He approached me and said you know what; I used to do the same thing as you. I gave him the time of day because he empathized with my predicament; we talked for roughly twenty minutes or so about God and A.A. I said if he could, I would be grateful for him to get me a Bible. He went out of his way and introduced me to a couple who I eventually stayed with for about three months.

I visited their house for the first time and they gave me the Living New Testament. They asked me to stay for a coffee, but I knew that the store would be soon closed for the night and I would miss out on getting some beer, so I respectfully declined the offer. Under a poorly lit lamp at night, I first started reading that Bible, I am so glad I did; even though I was drinking too.

I have many ideas that come into my head and if I don't have any paper, I just write Christ's words on my hand and then continue up my arm, I do not care what people think, I put God first now. The Lord somehow taps into my sub consciousness and changes its chemistry, keeps me positive, focused and reassured. He takes my best qualities and amplifies them ten fold, plus He keeps me calm and most importantly sober. Some people talk to God and hope He listens, however I not only speak to God, He speaks back to me, Praise the Lord. I believe this is the best Scripture to describe His power of preventing fear and anxiety inside of me.

Psalm 46:10: "Be still, and know that I am God"

I was offered by the Christian couple to stay with them as long as I didn't drink. I was extremely grateful for their generosity. I read the Bible regularly, listened to audio CD's about God, watched DVDs and attended the best church in the world with them. Now I attend a gospel church I also love, it is called Zion City Tabernacle.

Again I digress, I picked up a few jobs lawn mowing and tree lopping labouring; they were so nice that they did not charge me rent because they said the Lord provides them with all their needs. Because I did not drink, I soon saved the money up to go skydiving. I had wanted to do it all my life. 14000 ft and 200 km an hour, I thought nothing could beat that rush. Sex, drugs and rock and roll couldn't compare to the adrenalin rush that day. So I thought nothing could beat that, they had some friends strong in faith stay over for a few nights. A lady who was of English origin told me meeting God would beat that, I didn't believe her, I do now. Nowadays I feel as though I'm flying not falling.

When I do come into some money, I must not forget to tithe to Set Free ministries, that Christian organisation was the church that saved me spiritually the most and led me to Christ who saved my life again, eternally this time.

I used to believe that I could not sleep properly without lots of booze in my system. I would lie awake all night thinking about booze if I had not had enough to comatose me. Now I wake up feeling fresh and ready to face the challenges God has in store for me for the day, but I keep forgetting to say grace, I'll get the hang of it eventually.

I recall when I had my last bender on alcohol. I was lying on the kitchen floor surrounded by sick, sad, lonely, and depressed and crying my eyeballs out. I am under no illusion that Christ could see the state I got myself in that night.

One day in the hostel I drank half a bottle of wine to make me better at nine in the morning. My Aussie mate was picking me up for work setting up marquee tents. I drank the other half of my wine in the car. We set up the truck, then headed on our way to our first job, I am ashamed to say it was a kindergarten school, luckily enough the kids remained in the classroom.

I remember another occasion I had drunk far too much lager and I was ejected by four bouncers at this ex service man's club. I woke up in my hostel dormitory to a young Canadian lad screaming that I had wet the bed and it had come through the mattress on to him, I was soaked as well. I still do not know to this day whether I had a practical joke played on me with a bucket of water thrown over me or not. However though, given my previous history, I could not rule out the fact that he could have been right in what he had said, I am sorry to him if that was the case.

Another manic episode

I have come back down to earth today from another manic episode and had to see the doctor because I frightened anyone I had contact with. In the cold light of day and when I am well again, like I am now, I can review what made me ill. This time around it wasn't even alcohol induced either.

Some people only have one period of mania in their lives. I have had several.

It's not fun losing your mind, believe me. I didn't eat, I got very loud, and my mind was racing with grand ideas and I didn't consider other people's point of view, which I realise I need to start respecting.

I fell out briefly with my Mum claiming there's nothing wrong with me, but there was. Instead of alcohol and drugs, it was caffeine this time that made me ill. I drink bodybuilding energy drinks as a substitute for alcohol to get a high. They are similar to steroids but like other drugs and alcohol, I consumed them to the extreme.

On top of that I would drink at least ten cups of coffee a day, because the trouble with my Bi Polarity highs is that I don't want to come down. Sometimes it's as though bread and water are the safest option for the sake of my well being.

I went to church instead of work and was overcome by this feeling that I don't need money or alcohol anymore, ever. I still believe money is the root of all evil; however alcohol I can do without, but sadly in this world money I can not.

If I had hundreds of pounds that day, I know I would have given it to the same church again like five years ago. Technically though it was not my money, the six hundred pounds or so I gave the Vicar I had that day was not mine. I had walked out the bank with a two grand loan and I didn't have a job either, I was stealing in a way. I contributed to the country's financial downturn, but now I am bankrupt, I am facing the consequences, all I can say is I must have sold myself well to that bank manager as I got a credit card off him as well.

Oh, on top of that of course I was drinking and annoying everyone in pubs, I was lucky not to get hurt either, I wasn't right in my mind; I was sick and would not have been able to protect myself. However even though I had a distorted and deluded view on how to live life, I was giving money away to people in bars and being very annoying but not hurting anyone, only myself.

I still speak to the Lord every day, and I have had to repent for not keeping my promise to stop smoking.

The Vicar at a local church told me it's better to repent instead of feeling remorse for my actions. When I am high and manic, I should never promise anyone anything; especially Christ. I have also come to realise I have to work to put food on the table. I thought that's it, I have had enough, I don't want to work for a greedy company whose only concern is earning more and more money and is not concerned about the welfare of its own staff or so I thought in my head.

I reached a compromise in my mind and luckily still have a job even though I earn roughly the same as being on benefits. Nevertheless I have friends there, a lot more than I did when I was a drinker on the dole.

You can still serve the Prince of Peace without having to be penniless. For example if I was to make any money out of this book for instance, ten per cent will go straight back to God at the very least.

Realising the error of my ways

I am so sorry for getting manic and preaching to everyone who cares about me, telling them what to do with their lives according to the Bible. There is a scripture that warns of this:

2 Timothy 4:2: "Preach the word; be instant in season, out of season; reprove, rebuke, exhort with all longsuffering and doctrine."

In laments terms we should think and then think again and pick the appropriate time to talk about the Gospel.

The reason why God gave us two ears and one mouth is so we listen twice as much as we speak. I still have the mind of Christ, but still have many lessons to learn.

If I learn a lot more scriptures, I will have a better chance of being the Lord's servant; I know I am not ready yet. Even when I am ready, I will just show that I am a nice person who believes in God, no one would listen to me when I'm manic and judgemental anyway.

Matthew 7:6: "Give not that which is holy unto the dogs, neither cast ye your pearls before swine, lest they trample them under their feet, and turn again and rend you."

Sometimes you have to become wiser and change how you approach others.

Christianity and the Bible to some people is controversial and nonsense, to me though, it gives life and salvation to all those who read it. However I respect we are all different, and it would be a boring world if we were all the same after all.

Today I have been humbled by the Lord, I need to listen and study more, and I don't know everything and must have foolishly thought I did, for that I repent.

If I do ever come into money again, I will endeavour to tithe; Christ and his church have saved my soul time after time, plus I will pay people back what I owe them. I know if I was still drinking, that only the shopkeeper over the road would have the lot instead.

Bi Polar, me and the cure

It is not God's will for people to be sick and that is why He died on the cross and was resurrected by the Father of creation in order that we shall live.

Romans 8:2: For the law of the Spirit of life in Christ Jesus hath made me free from the law of sin and death.

I will endeavour not to forget that money has been the root of all evil in my life. Money can buy me alcohol from the store from as little as one pound for a bottle of white cider. Alcohol was my ultimate downfall, even when I didn't have one, it would constantly play on my mind. When could I afford it, what alcoholic potion could I purchase and when would I get it next. I would scour the house looking for change; I would go to great lengths like looking in between the sofa and underneath the beds. I would steal change lying around the kitchen, living room and worst of all—my Mum's bedroom. I am ashamed to say I would hysterically rummage around through both mine and my Mum's coat pockets just to get a drink. This is how the thief ruled supreme over me for years; however I have discovered the antidote, a far more potent and pleasant influential drug on me that rules over the enemy now and that's Jesus Christ, Praise the Lord.

James 4:7 : "Submit yourselves, then, to God. Resist the devil, and he will flee from you."

I returned to work as a fire-fighter about five months after jumping out that building. I progressed from being sick to being on restricted duties in a fire safety centre. My old boss worked there and he helped me stay in employment, plus it was nice to see a friendly face, many other employees couldn't trust me, but I cannot blame them.

I was sent to a physical rehabilitation centre to regain my health and fitness. I still thought there was an outside chance of sitting on the back of a fire engine again, it was never going to happen, I realise that now. I even convinced a top psychiatrist that I did not try to commit suicide for fear I would lose my glamorous career. In the cold light of day I realise the organisation has a duty to the public and they come first before me.

Even so I did not deserve what was to come, I felt like they were punishing me and of course I was still drinking heavily. I was sent back to fire training school and treated as a new recruit. It was wrong as I had been in the job for four years and was treated like a 'sprog' as they say in this game. One particular officer had it in for me and really made me feel worthless.

At the end of the week, I would go on a crazy drinking session, my Mum went away for the weekend, and I was single and well off financially. So I just drank and drank can after can of beer to relieve the stress but of course it made things in my life so much worse. I would drink up to twenty on a Sunday and still try to attempt passing the course starting on the Monday. I spent more time in the Station officer's office in trouble than on the training yard.

I put a grievance in against that inferior officer I have mentioned but it didn't matter. I got warning after warning and knew my job was coming to an end.

I went in one day and could not face a final warning and then still try and pass the course, I just couldn't do it, and I didn't have the power. In despair I phoned the union and they advised me to go sick with stress. Even my course leader spoke to me and said, get well first, then come back. But it didn't matter; my contract was terminated illegally anyway.

I continued with court proceedings but the fire service kept putting it off.

The trouble was that they had a convincing case against me, but my solicitor was certain they had broken the law. I stole my credit card and bank card back out of my Mum's purse and planned my escape from the country. My Mum had not long cleared the one thousand pound plus debt on it.

I ran off to New York to start a new life, missed the court hearing but my solicitor got me five grand back off them, but I was expecting a lot higher. I lent money off my Dad, Mum and three of my best friends promising to pay them back when I got my cheque. I still owe all of them to this day five years on; I hope they can forgive me but as God as my witness I will pay them all back.

I spent about thirty days in America instead of four; broke, lonely and hungry and without a passport; It was stolen off me by a bar owner and his giant bouncers because I couldn't pay for one beer, my card had been stopped through irregular spending. I spent the remainder of my time there looking for this one bar of which there were thousands like it. The worst thing was that I never even took a sip of that glass of beer, I walked to the British embassy but as usual with anything British it was closed.

Eventually with my Mum's financial help I got home very skinny, in the same shorts and t shirt I went in, an empty wallet and a broken phone. I did not know I had Bi Polar disorder and neither did my Mum, she kicked me out the flat for my terrible behaviour, I don't blame her either.

One of my dear female friends helped me out, she gave me a place to stay and a little job but I threw it back in her face, I was out of control, all I wanted was my cheque so I could, you guessed it, drink. I regret that instead of paying my friends and family back what I owed them, I blew my five thousand pounds in a matter of weeks on strippers, drugs and alcohol. Without even realising it, I was opening the door for satan to enter and ruin my life.

The negative side of Bi Polar disorder was taking a firm grasp on me; I was thinking abnormally and acting impulsively. I went to live at my biological dad's house and slept on the sofa but I was losing control of my sanity. I was listening to music loudly at five in the morning, writing my thoughts about God and my view on life. I read those notes years later and thought what I was thinking; I even went as far as posting my thoughts through friends' letter boxes. My band mates knew something was wrong with me; in fact it took a documentary entitled the secret life of a manic depressive for the penny to drop that I had a mental health problem. I even owe the narrator of that programme for my rehabilitation who is Stephen Fry who is also Bi Polar.

My behaviour was getting worse, there was this budgie in his cage, and I thought to myself how unfair it was that he should be locked up in a cage all day, so I set him free. My sister realised where my head was but my brother didn't, I couldn't blame him for getting angry now either. However, at the time I never wanted the bird to be incarcerated again, so I had thrown the budgie cage down the bottom of the garden where he couldn't find it. Things escalated, we got into an almighty row and I regret that I raised my fist, but I never hit him, I never would. My dad had been drinking the night before and he has problems as well. He got angry and lifted up a table, so I grabbed a chair, I thought we were going to hurt one another, but it was weird. We both discarded our weapons and we unpredictably hugged each other instead. The budgie sadly died weeks later.

Two wrongs do not make a right; I learned this lesson the hard way.

I found myself consumed full of hatred and anger towards the fire service for making me both physically and mentally sick from their treatment of me and especially after my near death fall. It cost the fire brigade roughly 250,000 pounds because after an investigation, they deemed about ten drill towers unsafe and they had to be demolished and then rebuilt. This was on top of all the training and wages they had invested in me. At one stage all forty of the training towers were knocked off the run because of safety concerns.

When my Bi Polar was at its most severe I kept visiting fire stations, and one officer reported me and I had a police log against me. I ended up at my female friends' houses who are still fire fighters and my old instructor phoned me and told me not to go to fire stations again. However I was so ill I did the opposite. I went to the main headquarters and they kept me talking on purpose while someone phoned the police. Four police officers in two cars pulled up, one officer asked my name, and I answered, and was told to sit in the back of a cop car once again.

I had a magazine with a picture of a military style line up with the perpetrators who I felt at the time made me sick; I had circled their faces and crossed out their names. I was Bi Polar after all, they let me go in the end and one particular copper must have empathized with me and told me to do it through the proper channels and offered me a lift to my car; however it was only ten yards away. I am eternally grateful that I never drank that night. In fact I think Christ must have warned me not to drink and drive, Praise the Lord again.

I was hellbent on revenge at the time, but not any more, the Lord has humbled me.

Scripture on revenge: Leviticus 19:18 "Thou shalt not avenge, nor bear any grudge against the children of thy people, but thou shalt love thy neighbour as thyself: I am the LORD."

The most humble of all was our good Shepherd;

Isaiah 53:7: "He was oppressed, and he was afflicted, yet he opened not his mouth: he is brought as a lamb to the slaughter, and as a sheep before her shearers is dumb, so he openeth not his mouth."

My brother died eleven years ago; I know he and my Dad now are in heaven at peace with Christ, regardless of what I have been told by another Christian. He did not consider how I would feel—to think that my loved ones are in hell. They were both perfect examples of what a good person should be like on this planet.

If they could not make it into heaven then I felt no one should. It got me so angry and sick that I was considering walking away from God for the second time of my life. However, I thought no, why l should allow the comments from one man ruin my faith even though he was quoting true scripture. I decided then never to return to that Church or his house again but I wonderfully changed my mind and thanks to Jesus I forgave him and still do.

They both believed there was a God and both put other people before themselves. They were unselfish and I am blessed to have had them in my life, my family feel the same. Our heavenly Father did the most unselfish act of all:

1 John 4:9-12: "By this the love of God was manifested in us, that

God has sent His only begotten Son into the world so that we might live through Him. In this is love, not that we loved God, but that He loved us and sent His Son to be the propitiation for our sins. Beloved, if God so loved us, we also ought to love one another. No one has beheld God at any time; if we love one another, God abides in us, and His love is perfected in us."

Once I was so deluded and mixed up in my mind, that I was certain beyond doubt that I was God (sorry again Lord for that). I even had the crazy notion I was a millionaire and I was going to become a famous rapper or singer, even though I cannot rap or sing to save my life. I also thought it was my destiny to save the world one day, maybe it is still.

Owing to the fact that I had become a millionaire, I told other people how to become one like me.

My brother told me, you become a millionaire first and then tell me how to become one. I even took it as far as writing my foolproof plan down on paper and giving what I thought was the ultimate gift to others that I would meet just about anywhere.

My crazy theory was—get a load of credit cards from different banks, pay one off with the other and keep doing so until you are rich.

You know what though, now I do feel like a millionaire with Christ at my side,

I just got the method wrong before when I used to serve money and alcohol as my God.

Let nothing disturb you;
Nothing dismay you;
All things pass,
But God never changes.
Who ever has God Lacks nothing:
If you have only God,
You have more than enough.
Raymond C. Neale copyrighted 2006

My delusion that I was God was all due to the fact that some young gentleman was wearing a belt with the words Jesus loves you, inscribed on it and now I look back, I believe his belt speaks the truth in abundance and I was meant to see those words.

After seeing his belt, I got an almighty rush and high, I had about 500 pounds on me, so I just gave it all away, starting off by throwing twenty-pound notes at the DJ. This was all down to booze and finding an ecstasy tablet on the pavement in town. I knew exactly what was in the plastic bag so I just took it and came up on the train to that major city, where I knew there was a banging nightclub open in the morning.

The previous night I was in a strip club and I gave 150 pounds for cocaine and a night in a certain girl's company, if you know what I mean. But because of my manic depression, I finally came down from my high, and I was left exhausted and returned back to my hotel room alone and I never saw that stripper again or got my money back, good I do not want them now.

In this strip club I was so overcome by lust, on two occasions that I can remember, I had two girls dance for me at the same time. In fact I told the one dancer she was God (sorry again Lord) and she replied "yes I am".

I had to negotiate a long flight of steps to this particular gentleman's club.

I used to call it to myself, the stairway to heaven, I realise now it was the gateway and trapdoor to satan's lair and hell.

On another occasion I found this bar, I gave away my money away to anyone that was in my vicinity. I then foolishly returned there thinking they would look after me when I was penniless. Because I had no money to buy a round of drinks, one particular man took offence to me sitting at his precious table, so he ripped off my deceased brother's dog tag from around my neck. At the time I thought they were tough hard men, not anymore, the only one I fear now is God.

I recall in the same nightclub I thought I was God, I had tipped the bar staff twenty pounds each. I had given all of my cash away, so I asked for them to buy me a drink, they did so, reluctantly. Also I would threaten bank managers for not giving me any more money. I even walked out of a store with a contacted phone worth 400 pounds with no consideration on how I would pay it back considering I was jobless after all.

The day I fled to Northern Ireland was a day before I had an interview for cabin crew with a top airline company. At the time, that would have been my dream job, but now I really do have my dream job, I am proud to be employed by God.

When I worked for the thief, I was so fickle, restless and impulsive, I made snap decisions. In fact; if I would have waited half an hour or so, I would have had my new bank card, and I would not have had to go through the experience I did in Ireland, but now I am glad I did.

It is because of the experiences God has shown me so far and continues to do so, that I no longer fear the devil and all the traps he sets on this earth. I will go as far as to tell the whole world not to fear him. I have been given a God given talent that makes me tenacious and relentless for the greater good. I received it from Lord Jesus Christ and I thank Him again.

I am getting off the point, but I also think music was intended to be free,

God created it after all, that's why King David was such a talented musician back in biblical times. However thanks to a couple of certain legal internet sites, it is free and accessible to all people, if they gain access to an internet connection and a computer.

I have gone as far as deleting all the music I have downloaded of torrent sites because I was stealing, the only music left after deleting thousands of tunes was my own band's material; we go by the name of LOGAN. In fact I went into Sony Music Corporation in New York City to get us signed but I got the wrong building and I think I was too impatient to wait for directions to the correct premises.

I foolishly made the biggest mistake of my life believing that I was proud to be Bi Polar and I am so sorry to have ever thought it. If I would have got that statement published as it was I would have dishonoured Jesus Christ.

Mental health illness of any kind is a sickness of the mind, again I repent. Last week at a Christian music festival in Cornwall, I woke up one morning in my tent with this overwhelming feeling that I no longer needed to take medication and I have today thrown away all my tablets.

Now I have to prove to my doctors that Jesus' heavenly hands have healed me once and for all.

Now I am proud to say that Lord Jesus Christ has healed me of all mental health problems and has blessed me with a sound mind.

My history of mental health problems is horrific to say the least, the Lord has completely zapped them away and I thank him from the bottom of my heart.

Isaiah 53:4-5: Surely he took up our infirmities and carried our sorrows, yet we considered him stricken by God, smitten by him, and afflicted. But he was pierced for our transgressions, he was crushed for our iniquities; the punishment that brought us peace was upon him, and by his wounds we are healed.

I will return to my mental health doctor and this time I will tell him to sign me off and I will not take no for an answer. Praise Jesus all over again, I am so thankful and I pray for His forgiveness on this matter. The best way I can pay Him back is to sin no more.

John 8:10-11: When Jesus had lifted up himself, and saw none but the woman, he said unto her, Woman, where are those accusers? hath no man condemned thee? She said, No man, Lord. And Jesus said unto her, Neither do I condemn thee: go, and sin no more.

I am no longer Bi Polar or an alcoholic, Lord Jesus Christ has saved me. Please believe me when I say that He is real and all He asks is for people to believe in Him and to sin no more. I have discovered that He is the light, the way and the truth and His way is the best by far and that is why He died so that we would live through Him.

Mathew 8:17: This was to fulfil what was spoken through the prophet Isaiah: "He took up our infirmities and carried our diseases."

Jimi Hendrix once yelled out on stage "does anybody know the truth"—I do, his name is Jesus Christ and He is alive and the only Son of God.

Jesus lives in me

The Bible teaches that even if we have had tough times throughout our existence, if you strive for excellent morals, live a Godly lifestyle and do good for others on Earth and believe in Jesus as our Lord and saviour, then heaven is indeed in reach for all of us.

Matthew 5:10: "Blessed [are] they which are persecuted for righteousness' sake: for theirs is the kingdom of heaven."

None of us are perfect, especially me so I asked for forgiveness for my sins and continue to do so. I pursued Christ and was blessed to receive the gift of the Holy Spirit. I have never been so pleased about anything in my life.

The thief has caused me to go mad three times; nearly killed me three times, broke my nose three times, shattered my elbow, broke my femur bone in my leg, fractured my pelvis and collapsed my lung. He has left me bankrupt and given me a criminal record which I have recently burnt in the name of Jesus Christ our Lord in heaven. He endeavoured to destroy me with manic depression, OCD, paranoia and a sense of ultimate fear.

The thief comes only to kill, steal and destroy; God is of love, power and a sound mind. I revisited the place where I almost met my Maker since then. I found myself looking up at the tower and left baffled by how I am still breathing. At first I thought I was just very lucky, but if that was the case, I would have some sort of recurring physical health problems but I'm fine. In fact I am never better since Jesus Christ healed me yet again last month. I can walk, run and enjoy life to the full. I even still have all my teeth, there's not a suspicion in my mind now that what happened to me that day was a miracle. There have been many others since then too.

I am finding it hard to believe, but I can talk to God. In fact I don't want to say satan's name any more now; I will only try to refer to him as the thief or the father of lies, because that's all he is, he is nothing. I am humbled finally by God's presence, eventually I don't want to sin any more and if I do, I will repent. My only boss I serve now is the Lord Yarshua and I will endeavour to obey every word He tells me and help anyone in this world make it to heaven because I don't want to lose this precious gift I am honoured to have received.

John 16:13, 14: "Howbeit when He, the Spirit of truth, is come, He will guide you into all truth: for He shall not speak of Himself; but whatsoever He shall hear, that shall He speak: and He will show you things to come. He shall glorify Me . . ."

Wars, poverty and worldwide uprisings are caused through money, racism and misplaced religion. Whether you are rich or poor, black or white, Christian or Muslim, we all bleed the same colour and we are all descendants of Abraham no matter what religion you belong to, we are all in the bloodline of Christ.

Galatians 3:16: "The promises were spoken to Abraham and to his seed." The Scripture does not say "and to seeds," meaning many people, but "and to your seed," meaning one person, who is Christ.

By reading the Bible, I made a connection with God. I searched for the King of king's help, confessed him as my Lord, got baptised, read the Bible and received the Holy Spirit. Anyone can do it.

I believe that the following carnal sins are letting the thief rule our lives: lust, gluttony, pride, sloth, wrath, envy and greed. I have been guilty of every one but Jesus opened my eyes now to all seven. In this world it's near enough impossible to avoid them. I have decided to limit my exposure to them and make a concerted effort with God's help to avoid their inducing lure of temptation.

Lust–the media, sexual assault, being unfaithful to your partner, adultery, strip clubs, lustful masturbation, fornication, one night stands resulting from drunken night club experiences, pornography on the internet, DVDs and magazines.

Glamour model industries and adult television.

Pride— the media, vanity, constantly concerned with appearance, fashion shows, the red carpet, arrogance about how good your body looks, plastic surgery and expensive jewellery. All of which leads to ignorance of Christ.

Sloth— the media, apathy, watching too much TV, laziness, not willing to work anymore or just not working to your full potential.

Envy— the media, jealousy about what other people have in their lives and not appreciating what they already have. Other peoples money, jobs, sexual organs, body types and how others' lives seem better than their own. Gossip magazines, and finally the Press all cause us to have the green eyed monster in our souls.

Greed— gambling, the media, banks, giant corporations, willingness to walk over someone else just to further your own career to have a more comfortable life and be a slave to money. You can't serve money as your master and God at the same time, you just can't.

Wrath— war, terrorism, hate, anger, fighting, domestic violence, bullying, road rage and murder.

Gluttony—greediness, take-a-ways, lack of exercise, TV dinners, fast food and blatant disregard for one's health. These are all the works of the thief and are poignant to my next topic.

I am no longer simply just interested in the carnal, material and superficial things in life. I am going to put all my trust in the Lord; I'll go as far as to say I would die happily tonight after my awesome experience with Him. I shall let God's angels minister for me from now until eternity.

Jeremiah 17:7: "Blessed is the man who trusts in the Lord, and whose hope is the Lord."

My main consideration and focus from now on is to tell the world that Jesus Christ loves us all and walks amongst us because I have been given the gift of the mind of Christ. The other main consideration I have is the health of my family and my true friends then every other creature on earth.

When I can afford it, I would like to willingly start tithing ten per cent of whatever I earn to the church because that's what the Bible teaches and above all I want to.

2 Corinthians 9:7 "Each man should give what he has decided in his heart to give, not reluctantly or under compulsion, for God loves a cheerful giver."

A song has just come on from 2 Pac, one of my favourite rappers, a music artist who died years ago, it is called staring at the world through my rear view, that's how I feel now. I am part of God's plan and that is why I was never going to die until I served my purpose in life to become God's messenger and tell the whole world about the glory of God and that His name is Jesus Christ.

If I can save one person from experiencing hell on earth, I will have done it by delivering the good news that Jesus Christ is real. In fact it's the year 2011 and the date today is laid down by the blood He shed the day He died, His resurrection to heaven and return to the Father. He has manifested His glory to me so that I may type this right now. We are still in the 27th book of the Revelation, of Jesus Christ, the last book in the Bible.

He enlightens me to appreciate the amazing world in which we live in, and commands me not to succumb to sin. This testimony is revelation of how to resist the thief on earth; there is a far greater reward waiting in heaven that is far beyond anything I can obtain on earth.

Hallelujah, Hosanna in the Highest, Praise the Lord. Nothing is higher than the Son, the Father and the Holy Ghost and the Word which is freely available to everyone on this globe.

I am 100 per cent certain the chaos that has spread through the world was all because Adam ate the apple of knowledge in the Garden of Eden all those years ago and unleashing the evil that comes from the enemy and the father of all lies.

I will endeavour to obey the Bible from now on, because after all we are all sinners! If only the world would listen to God and worship Christ we could have the strength of mind and power to save this world from ultimate destruction.

That is until Jesus Christ returns to this world in all His glory and very soon He will.

God's plan for me

John 14:6: "Jesus answered, I am the way and the truth and the life. No one comes to the Father except through me."

My life on Earth is not all I live for nowadays, I would love to make it into heaven. I know my best chance of reaching the Promised Land is through maintaining a good strong faith in Jesus Christ.

I repent to Saint Paul as well, I disagreed with some of his teachings in the New Testament which incidentally he wrote the majority of. I cursed his name, I am sorry and I hope he forgives me.

The fear of losing God's supernatural gift that He gave me is all the encouragement I need to commence living a holier life, with the apostles and the saints as my role models and most importantly Jesus. Once at Bible study, I alleged that it would be impossible to do, but now I have I changed my mind and I repent. When I make mistakes I will remember to simply say sorry to Him above, either by mouth or in thought.

I understand that non believers would find this all hard to believe, but if you would have witnessed how bad I became and how ill I looked before the Lord rescued me, you might believe me then. I was in a very dark place, suicide would have been the next stage, thinking it would be my only option out; I am sure of that. It is all academical now because Christ saved me, but I spare a thought for the families and friends of those who have lost loved ones through suicide like my family and to those who gave their lives for our country. God save the Queen.

Whenever Christ gives me inspiration which He does regularly; I make a sign of the cross, kneel down and point to the sky or all three as a thank You to Him.

God did not create me to become a raging alcoholic but to be well and live my life abundantly. I was saved by Jesus and He also knows my future too. I can't hold back water; it will keep flowing where it wants to flow. In other words, what will be, will be? Amen means so be it. I am still not too old to become more athletic or even become an amateur bodybuilder, anything is now possible with God in my life, and I know that for sure.

𝕸atthew 19:26: "𝕵esus looked at them and said, 𝖂ith men this is impossible, but with 𝕲od all things are possible."

My new holy like lifestyle will cast out satan by me adhering to Jesus' Commandments outlined in the New Testament of the Bible, all of which is the Word of God. I just speak His words not mine to command the enemy to flee I read the Bible more regularly if I am able to, even though I honestly struggle to understand some teachings inside it: I still believe, in fact I know, it's real, every word of it.

𝕵ohn 1:1 "𝕴n the beginning was the 𝖂ord, and the 𝖂ord was with 𝕲od, and the 𝖂ord was 𝕲od."

Jesus has already healed me 2011 years ago and because I was killing myself, He has had to do it again recently, well He didn't have to; but wanted to. You would think He would grow tired of helping me but no, I cannot say thank You to Him who created me enough. He is in my eyes, especially after my recent encounter with Him, my only Boss, King of kings, Lord God almighty. My Redeemer lives.

I will pursue Christ more, He has always followed me, carried me and I am certain He will show me a better path to walk along for the rest of my life. I am eternally grateful.

Footprints in the Sand

One night I dreamed I was walking along the beach with the Lord.
Many scenes from my life flashed across the sky.
In each scene I noticed footprints in the sand.
Sometimes there were two sets of footprints,
Other times there were one set of footprints.

This bothered me because
I noticed that during the low periods of my life,
when I was suffering from anguish, sorrow or defeat,
I could see only one set of footprints.

So I said to the Lord,
"You promised me Lord,
that if I followed you,
You would walk with me always.
But I have noticed that during
the most trying periods of my life
there have only been one
set of footprints in the sand.
Why, when I needed you most,
You have not been there for me?"

The Lord replied,
"The times when you have
seen only one set of footprints,
is when I carried you."

When I hear the words: praise the Lord, glory to God, Hosanna and Hallelujah; I get excited about praising God. That is the style of preaching from pastors and churches I liked before I even searched for Christ. So I was fortunate in that sense that the church I frequented in Australia was like that, and even had a live band performing.

Being a recreational musician myself, it was absolutely perfect for my individual personality. I still never fell over though like the rest of the congregation, maybe I was never destined to tumble the day when I confessed Him as my Lord?

Romans 10:9: "If you declare with your mouth, "Jesus is Lord," and believe in your heart that God raised him from the dead, you will be saved."

A lot of people do not believe in God because they question why bad things happen in the world. I consider it is because of how modern society has been shaped by the evil thoughts of unholy men, bad ideas come from satan not God. I know this because of what has happened in my life. Under the influence of drink and drugs about five years ago, I used to hear voices in my head constantly repeating the words "kill yourself Craig, kill yourself" I tried and I couldn't do it, thank God. I bet the thief planted those thoughts in my mind; he is after all deceitful, wicked and deadly. Nowadays I only mention the name of Jesus, and he is left quivering and shaking in his boots. Zion City Tabernacle taught me that one, Praise the Lord.

James 4:7: "Submit yourselves, then, to God. Resist the devil, and he will flee from you."

I am so happy I never took any more tablets than a hundred, and that I couldn't get to the twentieth floor of that high rise building that day.

Manic depressives tend to be talented in art but troubled; Some movie stars, pop stars and artistes just to name a few, have had, and still have Bi Polar. My concentration and positive attributes are beginning to shine since Christ healed me of my Bi Polar dissorder.

I write down all on paper, type and even scribble on my hand any good ideas the Lord gives me, I find it fascinating. I have a new-found interest in my bass guitar, weight lifting and music all of which the thief took away with manic depression, drunkenness and anxiety. Two female fire-fighters I met at fire training school became great friends of mine and have given me invaluable support over the years. They told me about the six P's they are: planning, preparation and perseverance prevents poor performance, they were right.

Hebrews 11:6: "God is a rewarder of them that diligently seek him."

I never believed it before but I recognise that God sees all and knows everything about me, He is the creator of all life and only He decides when mine ends. It is already written for me.

I have experienced what life the thief has to offer and believe me, he is nothing. There is no greater power on this Earth than the Holy Trinity. I am blessed in the name of the Father, the Son and the Holy Spirit. Amen.

My faith has never been so strong and powerful in Christ. My favourite pastors who are both male and female who introduced me to Jesus say the following phrase:

"The thief knocked at the door, faith answered and there was nobody there."

Even though it's not Biblical, I like it.

Christianity has worked for me

Maybe it hasn't worked out for everyone who has tried faith, but I can genuinely say that Christianity has worked for me. I want to attend church regularly to worship Christ, but I do not necessarily have to, I talk to Him on a daily basis and study the Word but not enough yet.

I feel as though I can never do enough for Him to right my wrongs, and repay Him for continually saving my life but I am going to give it my best shot.

I try to remember to pray to Him every day in my own unorthodox little way. I believe in the Cross, and believe He bore our sins over two millennia ago. I accept all of my character defects and I am making a concerted effort to change.

By doing this, I am beginning to eradicate the thief's grip on my personality and overall potential.

I accepted Christ as my Lord, Saviour and Redeemer and asked for forgiveness of my iniquities. As part of my rehabilitation programme in A.A, I also need to apologise to all the people I have hurt in drink in the past.

I have read all sixty six books of the Bible bar one hundred or so pages. I started with John then read the rest of the New Testament, after that I read the Old Testament. Only trouble was a year ago I started to get frustrated and at times angry with some of its teachings. I thought no, I'm not that naive to accept that not any more, every word of the holy Bible is true.

Christ has healed me of all sickness, suffering and disease; He answered my cry for help and I wish to honour the God's Commandments.

The Ten Commandments in brief and how they affect me:

Put God first—No problem with this one whatsoever.

Worship God only—Same again, no 'problemo'

Use God's name with respect—I am not finding this one difficult either.

Remember God's Sabbath—On Sundays I worship at a fantastic Gospel type church. No work for me any more on this particular day unless I do a Christian act, I just want to worship Christ, every day in fact. Jesus along with fantastic support from my friends and family has continually saved me from falling. God only asks me for one day a week to remember Him by, I appreciate that this is not much to ask for especially compared to what He has given me in return.

Respect your parents—Now that I have stopped drinking, my Mum is glad to finally have her son back, so is my big brother happy to have his younger bro back. Incidentally. apart from Jesus, they are the two I respect the most in this world alive. I am also rebuilding a relationship with my biological father, half brother and sister. My Dad was supposed to get married to his partner and she tragically lost him to a heart attack: I respect her so much I now call her my stepmother.

Do not hurt (kill) other people—I only used to upset others emotionally, not physically and I never really meant to. Even so I know it was wrong, but I am also aware that I have good qualities in me and a lot of my actions were again down to alcohol. I could definitely never take someone's life away; I feel guilty even when I kill a fly.

Be faithful in marriage—Again, now I have stopped drinking, one day, I shall meet a potential bride, marry her and then stay faithful to her.

Do not steal—I mainly did this on some occasions for money for drink and even then it was pennies or pounds lying around the house, now I would never dream of doing that.

Do not lie—This law is the only one I am going to struggle with, in this world, honesty especially at work can get you into trouble. I will try not find myself in situations that I would be tempted to lie, Ultimately I probably will lie and will remember to repent when I do so.

Do not be envious of others—I don't know what has happened to me, well actually I do it's Jesus Christ. I was a bad offender of this law. But now I am not bothered by what other people have got that I haven't, I am glad to be healed of jealousy.

My covenant with Jesus Christ right now is to try to adhere to these laws at the very least. I hope God will forgive me for not agreeing with or understanding other areas taught in the Bible in the past, I am not perfect after all and God is well aware of that. I don't want to walk away from Him again.

I would be a hypocrite to preach the word of God as I do not fully understand every word of the Good Book. Nevertheless I hope by writing this testimony and telling my story I might reach someone in need in this world. One thing I can assure Christ is that I will carry on His good works, spread the good news that Jesus is alive, and overall just be a better person, for the sake of my God, my family, friends and I.

Heaven help me

The Old Testament teaches me to put God first before anything else, even my family.

Exodus 20: 2-17: "I am the Lord your God, which have brought you out of the land of Egypt, out of the house of bondage. You shall have no other gods before me." You shall not make unto you any graven image, or any likeness of any thing that is in heaven above, or that is in the earth beneath, or that is in the water under the earth: You shall not bow down thyself to them, nor serve them: for I the Lord your God am a jealous God, visiting the iniquity of the fathers upon the children unto the third and fourth generation of them that hate me; And showing mercy unto thousands of them that love me, and keep my Commandments.

The Old Testament goes on to state that I should worship God only. I have many people who inspire me with the talents they possess, but I am also aware where their talents and skills came from in the first place.

You shall not take the name of the Lord your God in vain; for the Lord will not hold him guiltless that taketh his name in vain.

I now use God's name with respect. I do not use it for irrelevant and unimportant things any more and I certainly don't use the Lord's name in vain.

Remember the sabbath day, to keep it holy. Six days shall you labour, and do all your work: But the seventh day is the sabbath of the Lord your God: in it you shall not do any work, you, nor your son, nor your daughter, your manservant, nor your maidservant, nor your cattle, nor your stranger that is within your gates: For in six days the Lord made heaven and earth, the sea, and all that in them is, and rested the seventh day: wherefore the Lord blessed the sabbath day, and hallowed it. Remember God's Sabbath. Honour your father and your mother: that your days may be long upon the land which the Lord your God giveth you.

I realise now God is abundantly more important than money which is a by product of satan in my eyes. I no longer want to get stressed and tired at work to earn poor money at that. My Sundays will be more peaceful from now on. In fact I want to be seated in the pews of my own personal favourite and most beautiful churches I know, in this country anyway.

Respect your parents, honour your father and your mother: that your days may be long upon the land which the Lord your God giveth you.

Possessed by the demon drink, I did not follow this law. I thought I did but since the love of Christ has come over me, I don't just love my parents, I respect them and honour them.

You shall not kill.

I do not hurt other people any more. Don't get me wrong Christ has given the wisdom to see better, and bravery to stop people walking all over me. Christ in the eyes of some is that He is soft. I experience His supernatural powers, He is all loving but He is no mug, just one drop of His blood is way tougher, stronger and more supreme than anyone who walks this earth.

You shall not commit adultery. I cannot exactly follow this yet, I need to find a willing potential bride, marry her before I can remain faithful in marriage.

You shall not steal. I do not steal any more. I am not keen on others doing it either.

You shall not bear false witness against your neighbour. I will endeavour not to lie.

You shall not covet your neighbour's house; you shall not covet your neighbour's wife, or his manservant, or his maidservant, or his ox, or his ass, or any thing that is your neighbour's. Do not be envious of others.

Christ gave me the power of solace, serenity and peace. I don't get jealous over anyone any more or of anything. How can I possibly get envious of others with God in my life?

I continue to follow Christ, He has always followed and protected me; I believe He is the light, the truth and the way to salvation.

Jesus Christ and the words He spoke in the gospel are the only way to cast out demons and the enemy. Jesus spoke and the enemy fled. The disciples and apostles did the same. Jesus told them to do it and they did, so I do too.

Mark 16:15-18: And he said to them, "Go into all the world and proclaim the gospel to the whole creation. Whoever believes and is baptized will be saved, but whoever does not believe will be condemned. And these signs will accompany those who believe: in my name they will cast out demons; they will speak in new tongues; they will pick up serpents with their hands; and if they drink any deadly poison, it will not hurt them; they will lay their hands on the sick, and they will recover."

Messages

John 1:1. "In the beginning was the Word, and the Word was with God, and the Word was God." KJV

John 10:10: "The thief cometh not, but for to steal, and to kill, and to destroy: I am come that they might have life, and that they might have it more abundantly." KJV

2 Timothy 1:7: "For God hath not given us the spirit of fear; but of power, and of love, and of a sound mind." KJV

Psalm 46:10: "Be still, and know that I am God: I will be exalted among the heathen, I will be exalted in the earth." KJV

Exodus 3:14 "God said to Moses, 'I AM WHO I AM.' This is what you are to say to the Israelites: 'I AM has sent me to you.'" NIV

Isaiah 53:5: "But he was wounded for our transgressions, he was bruised for our iniquities; the chastisement of our peace was upon him, and by his stripes we are healed." KJV

Jeremiah 1:5: "Before I formed you in the womb I knew you, before you were born I set you apart; I appointed you as a prophet to the nations." NIV

I want to spread the good news of Jesus.

I listen with the two ears God gave me, and pay attention to how the thief can steal kill and destroy anyone's life if they let him. However, the thief isn't worth talking about.

One drop of Christ's amazing blood is far more powerful than the father of lies. I feel incredible and I do not want another alcoholic drink again. In alcohol, my lights were on but there was nobody at the inn, except the thief of course knocking at my door. Now, with Christ in my life . . . the thief knocks at the door, faith answers;

And there is no one there.

After I lost my amazing job as a fireman, I was distraught. My favourite aunty told me at the end of the day it is just a job. These words resonate in my brain still to this day.

I finished my temporary contract at work and matters could have got a whole lot worse, so I am willing to volunteer at a local church, and hopefully work officially for the Lord, in fact I do.

When I eat, I simply say, thank you Lord for Mother Nature, you are too kind.

My life is precious and I have and us all only one go at making it into heaven.

To taste the sweetness of God, I have had to suffer pain from the thief.

I owe my whole life to our Saviour and Redeemer Jesus Christ.

He has given me this one moment in time to get his words to all nations I hope.

He never fully manifested himself until I decided not to drink anymore.

I would go as far to say that I have drunk enough alcohol to sink a boat.

Only I never drowned because Christ held out his hand, and He alone pulled me out of the dangerous waters.

I cling on to His healing hands for dear life.

Thank you Lord for your never ending kindness and family and friends You blessed me with.

Incidentally the name of the man who first led me to the Lord shares the same name as my Father I had on earth and now in heaven.

I will remain obedient to God as best I can because I do not want to lose the wonderful gifts He has stored upon me.

𝔍𝔬𝔟 1: 20-21: "𝔗𝔥𝔢𝔫 𝔍𝔬𝔟 𝔞𝔯𝔬𝔰𝔢, 𝔞𝔫𝔡 𝔯𝔢𝔫𝔱 𝔥𝔦𝔰 𝔪𝔞𝔫𝔱𝔩𝔢, 𝔞𝔫𝔡 𝔰𝔥𝔞𝔳𝔢𝔡 𝔥𝔦𝔰 𝔥𝔢𝔞𝔡, 𝔞𝔫𝔡 𝔣𝔢𝔩𝔩 𝔡𝔬𝔴𝔫 𝔲𝔭𝔬𝔫 𝔱𝔥𝔢 𝔤𝔯𝔬𝔲𝔫𝔡, 𝔞𝔫𝔡 𝔴𝔬𝔯𝔰𝔥𝔦𝔭𝔭𝔢𝔡,

And said, Naked came I out of my mother's womb, and naked shall I return thither: the Lord gave, and the Lord hath taken away; blessed be the name of the Lord."

I want to learn Spanish now so I can talk in different tongues and I feel it is Christ's wish for me. It is not exactly what the Bible teaches, but I think it's a positive start. My gift is writing, and I can talk for England now I am no longer depressed. Praise the Lord.

𝔐𝔞𝔯𝔨 16:15-18: 𝔄𝔫𝔡 𝔥𝔢 𝔰𝔞𝔦𝔡 𝔱𝔬 𝔱𝔥𝔢𝔪, "𝔊𝔬 𝔦𝔫𝔱𝔬 𝔞𝔩𝔩 𝔱𝔥𝔢 𝔴𝔬𝔯𝔩𝔡 𝔞𝔫𝔡 𝔭𝔯𝔬𝔠𝔩𝔞𝔦𝔪 𝔱𝔥𝔢 𝔤𝔬𝔰𝔭𝔢𝔩 𝔱𝔬 𝔱𝔥𝔢 𝔴𝔥𝔬𝔩𝔢 𝔠𝔯𝔢𝔞𝔱𝔦𝔬𝔫. 𝔚𝔥𝔬𝔢𝔳𝔢𝔯 𝔟𝔢𝔩𝔦𝔢𝔳𝔢𝔰 𝔞𝔫𝔡 𝔦𝔰 𝔟𝔞𝔭𝔱𝔦𝔷𝔢𝔡 𝔴𝔦𝔩𝔩 𝔟𝔢 𝔰𝔞𝔳𝔢𝔡, 𝔟𝔲𝔱 𝔴𝔥𝔬𝔢𝔳𝔢𝔯 𝔡𝔬𝔢𝔰 𝔫𝔬𝔱 𝔟𝔢𝔩𝔦𝔢𝔳𝔢 𝔴𝔦𝔩𝔩 𝔟𝔢 𝔠𝔬𝔫𝔡𝔢𝔪𝔫𝔢𝔡. 𝔄𝔫𝔡 𝔱𝔥𝔢𝔰𝔢 𝔰𝔦𝔤𝔫𝔰 𝔴𝔦𝔩𝔩 𝔞𝔠𝔠𝔬𝔪𝔭𝔞𝔫𝔶 𝔱𝔥𝔬𝔰𝔢 𝔴𝔥𝔬 𝔟𝔢𝔩𝔦𝔢𝔳𝔢: 𝔦𝔫 𝔪𝔶 𝔫𝔞𝔪𝔢 𝔱𝔥𝔢𝔶 𝔴𝔦𝔩𝔩 𝔠𝔞𝔰𝔱 𝔬𝔲𝔱 𝔡𝔢𝔪𝔬𝔫𝔰; 𝔱𝔥𝔢𝔶 𝔴𝔦𝔩𝔩 𝔰𝔭𝔢𝔞𝔨 𝔦𝔫 𝔫𝔢𝔴 𝔱𝔬𝔫𝔤𝔲𝔢𝔰; 𝔱𝔥𝔢𝔶 𝔴𝔦𝔩𝔩 𝔭𝔦𝔠𝔨 𝔲𝔭 𝔰𝔢𝔯𝔭𝔢𝔫𝔱𝔰 𝔴𝔦𝔱𝔥 𝔱𝔥𝔢𝔦𝔯 𝔥𝔞𝔫𝔡𝔰; 𝔞𝔫𝔡 𝔦𝔣 𝔱𝔥𝔢𝔶 𝔡𝔯𝔦𝔫𝔨 𝔞𝔫𝔶 𝔡𝔢𝔞𝔡𝔩𝔶 𝔭𝔬𝔦𝔰𝔬𝔫, 𝔦𝔱 𝔴𝔦𝔩𝔩 𝔫𝔬𝔱 𝔥𝔲𝔯𝔱 𝔱𝔥𝔢𝔪; 𝔱𝔥𝔢𝔶 𝔴𝔦𝔩𝔩 𝔩𝔞𝔶 𝔱𝔥𝔢𝔦𝔯 𝔥𝔞𝔫𝔡𝔰 𝔬𝔫 𝔱𝔥𝔢 𝔰𝔦𝔠𝔨, 𝔞𝔫𝔡 𝔱𝔥𝔢𝔶 𝔴𝔦𝔩𝔩 𝔯𝔢𝔠𝔬𝔳𝔢𝔯."

It is my opinion that mental health illnesses could simply be the thief trying to destroy Christ's good works on earth, and God will conquer that eventually and finally win. Of course though, I can only speak for myself on this particular matter.

I have been to about ten Alcoholic Anonymous meetings now, and I know why there's wonders worked in the room, the original serenity prayer had the name of Jesus Christ at the end.

The Lords' supernatural force and good works operate in A.A and I'm sure He's in Narcotics Anonymous too. Christ is aware that the sufferers in those rooms have already been through hell on earth. Maybe Jesus helps those in the room because they are helping themselves first.

Even without realising it and not asking Him for help, He offers His love and support. I and every other member of A.A are shown another much better way without having to suffocate the thief's asphyxiating strangulation.'

It would cost about one and half hours work just for two pints of lager/cider and whatever fags I would have to smoke as another drug to supplement it. I look back now and think what was I thinking and I have only been clean for four weeks.

It was easy too as me firstly picking up a book (the Bible) and then asking the Lord Jesus Christ for help and then He took it from there.

I have put all my trust in the Lord and everything has changed inside my heart for the better.

I have exchanged the thief's wicked way of thinking for the mind of Christ. I endeavour to walk the Lord's righteous path nowadays on my journey to heaven and my Abba Father. Personally, I have the Bible on audio and video for my PC, and it is like music to my ears. The words come alive, speak to me aloud and my mind absorbs it so much more and I read it on screen too.

I have a lot of respect for the music artist Mariah Carey and the song she wrote entitled Hero. My Hero is the Lord Jesus Christ for all He has done for me and times He has rescued me. Immanuel (God is with us) has written my entire life before I was even in my mother's womb. Praise God, Hallelujah, high and mighty.

I am not ashamed of the Gospel. Romans 1:16
Jesus is whiter, even more whiter than snow.
He has guided me from the storm.
Nothing on earth can beat or even compare to the love of God.
God bless Mother Nature and the Circle of Life.

There is nowhere for the thief to hide from the Father of all creation.

Learning to love the Lord is encouraging me so much, that I am learning to love myself as well. Whitney Houston was right all along, and she's a Christian like me and I bet she is proud of it, I certainly am. Christ has freed me from my burden of sin.

Rejoice in the name of the Lord and all his saints. What better role models could I possibly have?

Even when I do not know what's best for me, Christ does. He is gentle, considerate, He picks me up when I'm down and makes all my best decisions all day, everyday. He sometimes gives me a kick up the butt too, to get me more motivated. Jesus encourages me to be more enthusiastic to be alive; and after all "everyday above the ground is good day "or something along those lines. (Quote from 2pac Shakur.)

Jesus has given me such a power of wisdom, that I walk the streets in town and I can spot sin a mile away and I do not want it for me anymore.

He knows what music I have been brought up on and what my cup of tea is. He will guide me to playing 2pac, Bob Marley, Mariah Carey, Michael Jackson and Stevie Wonder to name but a few.

An Estonian girl from Eastern Europe once told me I was the best boy in the hostel in Cronulla, Sydney, Australia. She was like an angel to me and she also said if I do good things, I will have good things happen to me. Another angel God sent me was the girl from my home country's capital incidentally.

I do not just love Jesus; I have the upmost respect for what He did for me. I could never imagine the pain and torture He suffered during his flogging, mocking, having to carry his own cross and subsequent crucifixion. I believe the Word when it says He was sinless and still got punished as though He had brought terror into the world. However, the truth was the complete and utter opposite, Praise the Lord.

Alcohol abuse took my soul; Christ has restored it in abundance, Thank You God eternally, Lord, for being ever present in my heart, soul, spirit and my mind.

A nice lady from work once told me I have only one chance at life and that I should make the most of it. Life is indeed short and precious, I hope my efforts on Planet Earth will be sufficient to join my brother and father in heaven. The Lord has blessed with my brother's courage and my Father's wisdom. My brother was an infantry soldier in the British Army and my Dad was a very intelligent person in general.

I am adamant that I will respect the woman that the Lord brings into my life.

After all—hell hath no fury like a woman scorned. A girl not too far from me is an exception to this; she has accepted that I only want to be friends with her even though it was me who kept trying it on, all because I was under the influence of alcohol again. Oh and she believe in Jesus Christ too, bless her.

I began using alcohol for escapism from all of life's trials and tribulations.

I either drowned my sorrows, celebrated small victories or just drunk out of pure boredom, either way I would be drunk.

I recall I used to panic with fear if the store was about to close or I'd be absolutely terrified when it actually had. One of my cherished friends who's a police officer, took me out for a drink once, and even though I was glad to catch up with her, the first couple of drinks triggered off the monster in my head and I knew there were not going to be many more. I was relieved when it was past ten pm, so I didn't have to ask her to lend me some money to get some cider.

She along with other friends, family and colleagues from the fire brigade especially have given me invaluable support and kept my chin up during tough times. Christ has reminded me of those He has worked in to get me here today and I am eternally grateful.

I respect my Dad so much, I recall he used to drive a 25 mile round trip everyday for about ten weeks to see me in hospital and bring my Mum. Also they had recently separated, I realise it must have been so hard. I tried to return just a little bit of that support when he was recovering in hospital from a successful operation to re-attach his colon. I was told he was moved to critical care, and then the nurse took me to the relative's room. As soon as I saw my step-Mum and my two sisters crying, I feared the worst and I was then told he had passed away. It was tragic that he was going to marry this wonderful lady and be happy together from then on. He is sorely missed by all that loved him, He is not in pain any more and hopefully we will all get to see him again someday.

I understand the scripture: as I walk through the valley of the shadow of death.

A Canadian girl said I was the nicest man she had ever met; she would not have said that if she witnessed me only a month or so ago. She is also the only woman I have ever loved so far.

God rescued me and now I realise I have searched for Him my entire life.

My eldest brother said once that when I put my mind to it, it happens.

I am easily influenced rightly or wrongly, now I have the most influential figure in life, Jesus.

The saying goes, you can lead a horse to water but you can't make it drink,

Jesus Christ can if you only let Him.

I believe everything in life happens for a reason. It took me a life of sin to reach God, so I do not regret anything, but I will make it up to those I have done wrong to, and it is a long list to say the least.

Words alone can not express how much I love His love.

Christ Jesus I love You and He loves me too, He tells me everyday.

Conclusions

I have been blessed with a gift from God.

I believe music greats like Michael Jackson and James Brown also had gifts from God. Hip hop legends 5o cent and 2pac were shot several times in single attempts and survived. And both wear in their videos crosses on chains outside their clothes to symbolise they are believers, and to show they are blessed from God with such lyrical, musical talent.

My zest for life is back in abundance and I have never written so much in my life, I hope to stretch my new found talents to playing my guitar more, once this book is finally complete.

Thank You Jesus Christ who I know has seen and heard all things in my life.

I am now not just a drunken bum, but a new creation and a 'go getter', Praise the Lord.

God is a mixture of four things and more, it is fitting that sometimes I use these four Scriptures to fight of satan who I now know is real and not just a fantasy figure anymore. The four things are The Father, the Son & the Holy Spirit and also the Word.

1   The thief comes only to steal, kill and destroy.
2   God is power, love and a sound mind
3   Be still and know that (I am) God
4   My Name is (I Am) Who (I Am)

God's name (I am) is referred to three times and that's why the words are so powerful. I have since learned that speaking the name Jesus by mouth is all that is needed to frighten the enemy off. Jesus Christ healed us way back then and we are still healed now, talk to Him, He'll listen believe me.

I can't even begin to imagine how powerful He is in Heaven, I have only experienced a little bit of his glory.

I understand that Jesus had already healed me, but it seems I had to go on a journey before I met Him personally, now my faith is in overdrive and on fire. I am fully focused on my heavenly goals with the Lord's guidance and help of course.

I am a true believer in karma and faith, and what goes around comes around. I like to treat others how I would like to be treated nowadays. I also understand the phrase 'smile and the world will smile with you'. My grandmother was Irish, and when Irish eyes are smiling the world is forever gay.

I have mentioned a lot of my bad qualities, but now I will reflect on some of my good overall attributes Jesus blessed me with:
I am six ft one tall.
I am approximately 220 lbs I am reasonably handsome.
I am a good solid bass guitarist with 15 years experience playing in bands.
I am fit, strong and quite smart.
I am blessed with life experiences from God.
I am good at studying, planning & communicating, which means I am fine at job interviews.
I am charismatic, funny, and cheeky with lots to say.
I am independent and I do not fear going off halfway round the world on my own.
Christ guided me there to get saved after all.

I still have a text from my friend from London saying I do not have a bad bone in my body; there is something different about me. I now realise that 'something' is the presence of Jesus Christ and His eternal love.

I never had my life flash before my eyes before I blacked out 32 ft in the air. Neither did I remember anything when I was in a coma for four days. However since the Lord made Himself ever present in my life, some of my senses have become far superior to what they were. My mind is a lot sharper, wiser and I am way more focused. I felt one night that I was being elevated when clearly alive but half asleep, it was crazy, I asked the Lord not to take me yet because I didn't want my Mum to lose her other and final son.

It has been strange to get warm fuzzy feelings reverberating around my stomach but I welcome them all the same. My eyes get hazy and I get tunnel vision but it feels nice and when I write, I do not feel I am in control of the pen; it's like something out of Ghostbusters or something but real.

I can sense demonic forces and angelic spirits in my mind, it sounds bananas I know, but I really can. I am not on drink or drugs either anymore.

I have never felt better in my life; I do not worry about a thing. I am healed from the ultimate holy Doctor, Jesus Christ. Praise the Lord.

Why A.A has helped me too.

Original serenity prayer:

O God and Heavenly Father,
Grant to us the serenity of mind to accept that which cannot be changed; courage to change that which can be changed, and wisdom to know the one from the other, through Jesus Christ our Lord, Amen.

Living one day at a time;
Enjoying one moment at a time;
Accepting hardships as the pathway to peace;
Taking, as He did, this sinful world as it is, not as I would have it;
Trusting that He will make all things right if I surrender to His Will;
That I may be reasonably happy in this life and supremely happy with Him
Forever in the next.
Amen.

I went to visit the rector at St Peters today; it was ironic that it was directly opposite the strip club I used to frequent. Its new name is

(Sin)-derellas and that's exactly what it is. A fantasy tale starring naked ladies created by satan that killed me spiritually, Stole all my money and destroyed my intelligence, as I had lost the power of rational thought whilst drunk.

The thief targeted all my weak points, with his temptation of lust, alcohol, sex, drugs and rock n roll. All of which cost me a fortune to experience, and I never remembered half my exotic dances the next day either, I consider now what a waste of time and money it was to walk the road of the father of all lies.

A man once told me my situation is only as bad as my reaction to it. Before, I used to handle stress and work with drinking abundant amounts of alcohol and smoking ridiculous amounts of tobacco. But with the peace of mind which Christ offers me, I do not need any of that anymore, and more to the point I just do not want it.

I feel amazing; why on earth I would want to swap this for manic depression, anger, resentment, sadness, hate, misery and despair; the list goes on and on; I just wouldn't any more after all alcohol is a depressant.

I recommend to anybody of any faith to give Jesus Christ a try. The best things in life are free and the kind of love that the Lord offers is free, after all, there is nothing to lose and all so much to gain.

I may not have letters at the start of my name, a PhD or a diploma, I messed up university and currently do not have a job; however I study at the college of Christ, the most important and influential lessons in life are taught at this School.

The Pen is Mightier than the Sword

Hebrews 4:12-13 "For the word of God is living and active. Sharper than any double-edged sword, it penetrates even to dividing soul and spirit, joints and marrow; it judges the thoughts and attitudes of the heart. Nothing in all creation is hidden from God's sight. Everything is uncovered and laid bare before the eyes of him to whom we must give account."

The thief comes only to kill, steal, lie and destroy.
God is of love, and of power and a sound mind.
In the name of Our Heavenly Father,
The Word, the Son and the Holy Ghost . . .
Go back to where you came from.
You are the father all lies, sin and deceit.
There can be miracles when you believe in Our Lord in Heaven;
Jesus Christ;
Who is the Only Son Of?
I am That I am;
The true name of God who is genuinely real,
Eternally forgiving and never changes.
The Lord has always carried me in my life;
Because of the resurrection of Christ over two millennia ago.
Jesus paid the ultimate price by dying on the cross,
& shedding his blood to free us all from sin.
I am one of God's many miracles and I feel the Lord's power;
wonder working power in the blood of the Lamb. Amen

The thief invaded my soul with a sense of fear, money worries, a near deadly amount of alcohol, drugs and excessive smoking. He is to blame for all sickness and disease on this planet.

Tobacco plants originally come out the ground and are God's creation. However I believe smoking is bad for me because of all the chemicals that are added to make them more addictive. Both I, young and old people are hooked on cigarettes and as a consequence, spend far too much of their hard earned wages on them and also, already rich companies can make even more money.

These Scriptures I find keep the father of lies at bay.

John 10:10 & 2 Timothy 1:7: "The thief comes only to kill, steal and destroy. God has not given us the spirit of fear, but of love, power and a sound mind."

Psalm 46:10: "Be still and know that I am God."

Exodus 3:14 "His name is; I AM WHO I AM."

It is my belief that this entire world is consumed by terror, money, drugs, alcohol, violence and bad media. All of which are controlled by the thief with fear, lies, sin and deceit. Yarweh rebuke you.

I found out that God's Word is the solution to prevent him poisoning my soul again. I do not just read the Bible any longer, I try my best to live the Word of God in everyday life, it is amazing, and it really is. Since Jesus Christ entered me I have had a life changing experience, I urge anyone just to cry out the name of Jesus. Praise God.

Scriptures in full:

John 10:10-11: "The thief cometh not, but for to steal, and to kill, and to destroy: I am come that they might have life, and that they might have it more abundantly. I am the good shepherd: the good shepherd giveth his life for the sheep."

2 Timothy 1:7: "For God did not give us a spirit of fear but of love, and of power and a sound mind.

Psalm 46:10: "Be still and know that I am God."

Exodus 3:13-3:14: "God said to Moses, suppose I go to the Israelites and say to them. The God of your fathers has sent me to you, and they ask me, what is his name? Then what shall I tell them. God said to Moses, I AM WHO I AM."

Nowadays the only solitary being on this earth and in heaven that I fear Is God Almighty, Abba Father.

Ten Commandments I try to keep:

I Put God first, I have no other gods.
I do not worship idols, I only respect them.
I do not say the Lord's name in vain, I say sorry if I do . . .
I do not work on the Sabbath day any more.
I honour my parents.
I will not commit murder.
I will not commit adultery.
I do not steal, even pennies any more.
I try harder not to lie.
I do not envy anyone in this world anymore.
Jesus tells me to love others including my enemies as He has loved me

John 1; 1: "In the beginning was the Word, and the Word was with God, and the Word was God."

𝔐𝔞𝔱𝔱𝔥𝔢𝔴 4:4: "Jesus answered, "It is written: 'Man does not live on bread alone, but on every word that comes from the mouth of God.'"

𝔍𝔢𝔯𝔢𝔪𝔦𝔞𝔥 1:5: "Before I formed you in the womb I knew you."

𝔍𝔰𝔞𝔦𝔞𝔥 53:5 (𝕶𝔦𝔫𝔤 𝔍𝔞𝔪𝔢𝔰 𝔙𝔢𝔯𝔰𝔦𝔬𝔫)

But He was wounded for our transgressions,
He was bruised for our iniquities:
The chastisement of our peace was upon Him;
And with His stripes we are healed.
My actions will speak louder than my words and the more I do for God,
The more He does in return for me.

𝔍𝔞𝔪𝔢𝔰 4:8 𝕮𝔬𝔪𝔢 near to God and he will come near to you. Wash your hands, you sinners, and purify your hearts, you double-minded.

Jesus Christ helps me more when I help myself.
I realise now only Jesus can save me.
When I say grace—I say Thank You Lord for Mother Nature, You are too kind.
God operates within this world through people and places to accomplish his good works.
My reward for seeking Him is wisdom, strength, power and a rich enthusiasm to serve him.
I will enjoy my life in his glorious creation, planet earth.
Sin is dividing all kingdoms.
Christ will return all nations to Israel's Holy Land.
The Lord is all inspiring.
I say thank you to the Christ by making a sign of the cross, I kiss my cross and I point to the skies and speak, Praise Jesus or Praise the Lord, it's all good.
Hola . . .
When the Lord reminds me of a sin I committed in the past,

I get down on one knee and repent.

I have the best boss, doctor, teacher, friend and the most rewarding job in the entire universe.

Jesus Christ led me to Him and the Father of creation.

I confessed my sins and asked for His forgiveness.

I Praise the Lord every day now; I do not have to be in a church any more to talk to Him.

I stopped serving money as my master, and receive good things despite that.

Jesus is the truth, the light and the way to restore our wonderful world.

I utter the following Words when I feel the thief trying to worm his way into my soul:

"The thief comes only to kill steal and destroy.

God is love power and a sound mind." (Without me pausing for breath).

Then without delay I say:

"Be still and know that I am God" or "by His stripes we are healed".

Sometimes it needs one more I use "My name is I am who I am"

Oh and I round it all off now by simply declaring the name Jesus Christ, even Jesus will do. The enemy then flees to conjure up another plan to attack me with his evil, wicked ways.

The only way I can fight him is with faith, using the Word of Jesus Christ,

It is sharper than any double-edged sword or any other weapon on this planet.

Thanks to all my family, true friends and everyone that has helped me find peace in my mind and guide me into Christ's healing hands. I am more than a conqueror; I'm a new creation, I'm a brand new man.

A girl in a bar once said to me "if there were more people in the world like you, the world would be a better place". I feel honoured to receive such a compliment. In fact I feel like I'm top of the world and it's so much better than the bottom.

I now put Jesus first, then my family, then my friends, then work and then finally money at the bottom of my priorities.

I know I have received a gift from God who protects me so I can get my testimony out to the world. I am truly blessed from heaven. I hope my story may help believers grow stronger in there faith or make non believers believe; speak out to atheists or agnostics or anyone who doesn't know the full power and love Jesus offers to everyone, if only they seek His hand and learn to worship Him more, I do everyday.

I love Him more than anything else. I am no longer alone in this world; I have a friend for life and eternity. I did not have a religious upbringing, I have only been a member of the church for over a year, yet He is still my friend. He supports me; He gives me a shoulder to cry on and listens to every word I say. I can speak to Him anytime I need to; He is that loving and cares about every living thing on this planet. Above all, I truly believe He has forgiven me my sins.

I am proud to say that I have the greatest and most rewarding job in the world serving the Lord as my Master, instead of money. My supernatural gift from God is salvation given to me by grace through faith in our Lord Jesus Christ.

His only currency is to have faith in Him, the Holy Ghost, the Word and in the Lord, God Almighty, Abba Father, Creator of the heavens and the earth; I Am Who I Am.

God is the Father, the Son and the Holy Ghost, the last of which also goes by the name of the Holy Spirit. He dwells deep within the hearts of every believer in our Lord and Saviour Jesus Christ! The Holy Ghost that resides in me is deeply personal, treats me as an individual and attends to all my heavenly requirements and needs.

The Holy Ghost is indeed God inside of me; I watch out and hear for Him carefully, He tells me the enemy is nothing, to just say Jesus and he'll soon disappear! And He is right. The enemy can only feed off my fear, I learned of a lady in Alcoholics Anonymous that the opposite of fear is faith; my faith is on fire, a fire that is burning me with the Holy Spirit right now.

Jesus warns me of any wrongdoing and reveals to me the best course of action in all aspects of my life. I feel as though it is still me, I, Craig talking to myself, but the best possible Craig I can be.

Whenever I listen diligently to the voice within me, He guides me into becoming more righteous and more conscious and aware of my own faults and not those of others. He leads me from temptation and therefore I become less sinful in the eyes of my Redeemer, Lord, God, King Jeshua.

Matthew 26:41: "Watch and pray so that you will not fall into temptation. The spirit is willing, but the flesh is weak."

As I grow stronger in my Christian faith, I feel more confident, more obedient, less tempted and therefore more able to help teach the Gospel to others. Being Christian, written by Stephen Alterburn and John Shore was given to me from a lovely, godly lady from Set Free ministries, Rockdale, Sydney,

Australia. This book has helped me realise that the pain, hurt, misery and suffering that people experience in this world is not anything of God's doing but all of sinful man.

God gave us the magnificent gift of free will that unfortunately some men and women choose to abuse; and they use this gift for the works of evil instead of good. There is enough food on this beautiful planet of ours to feed all within it and enough water to quench everybody's thirst.

Universal love is what Jesus taught me to myself; to love not just my family and my friends but also any of my neighbours (I have no enemies nowadays). He taught me to love my neighbour regardless of their colour, creed or what continent they're from and whatever their social standing or background, their wealth, or what they possess that I do not. We are all God's creatures who walk upon His beloved creation.

This I can only do through Christ in my compliance with God's Word outlined in the Gospel. Now I have turned to Jesus, I communicate with Him regularly by reading the New Testament of the Holy Bible. I am also now more devoted to the Old Testament as it teaches me the rules of creation. Just reading the book of Saint John alone educates me about grace and love. Saint Luke, for me, sums it up best what the meaning of true love really is:

Luke 10:27: "He answered, Love the Lord your God with all your heart and with all your soul and with all your strength and with all your mind; and love your neighbour as yourself."

Jesus responded to the man and said:

𝕷uke 10:28 . . . "𝕯o this and you will live."

    I implore anyone to seek Christ in their lives; there is nothing to lose and only everything to gain. I am so glad I did; I have peace at last with the world.

    The father of creation and his Son Jesus Christ through the Holy Ghost; and through the friends and family He blessed me with, have taught me the true meaning of how to love and how to live. I also understand what it means to be a born again Christian and a child of Christ, I am one.

    Jesus walks with us, He really does.

𝕵ohn 3.33: "𝕳e who has received 𝕳is testimony has certified that 𝕲od is true."

    Jesus Christ has the most amazing testimony ever.

Poems

Oh heavenly Father,
Please forgive me all of my sins.
Lord of all Lords & the King of all kings;
Have mercy on my soul;
Heaven is where I wish to enrol.
Take me to the clouds above; the truth I long to know;
I am here for a reason He is I am that I am, I am going to be,
So . . .
Jesus Christ forever and ever.
Please fulfil my destiny. Amen Jesus Christ and Craig Harrison2011
I make mistakes, but try my best to learn from every one.
I'm a Soldier to the Father's only begotten Son.
I take Orders from the Lord. I'm living proof there's a God.
Christ's not finished with me yet . . .
His imminent return, Makes me happy we have met.
By far the love of Jesus Christ is the best that you can get. Amen

Jesus Christ and Craig Harrison2011

It all started when I lost my brother,
I'd lost faith in myself and trust in another.
Last resort for I Craig, was to find Immanuel (God is with us)
Because I know in my mind, I was headed to hell.
The bottom of the bottle was my one and only Lord,
I'm thankful to Christ, He Alone Cut the chord.
My love is now Strong,

'Cause the Lord is my Rock.
That's welsh interpret my name He who has always been mocked?
My God Jesus Christ guards the door,
If the thief, ever dare knock! Amen

Jesus Christ and Craig Harrison2011

You can not stop water,
It goes where it goes.
The Lord is my Sheppard And that much I know.
I get guidance from above,
His name is I am that I am.
His seed that I sow,
I get by the gram. Amen Jesus Christ and Craig Harrison2011
The world I see could be a lie; it serves money as its master.
As far as I'm concerned, Christ couldn't get here any faster.
Calvary washed me of my sins; and that much I know.
Every day with Lord Jesus Christ,
My spirit continues to Grow.

Jesus Christ and Craig Harrison2011

One drop of Christ's Blood is more powerful than him.
He is the father of all lies, and the creator of sin.
Jesus Christ and Craig Harrison2011
Since I discovered the Lord,
My life is not all about money.
God led me to a spiritual place,
Overfloweth with milk and honey.
By sowing a seed now,
I'm building a more improved future.
The better the seed that I sow The more I become nurtured.
I have captured God's anointing,
I want to be the best that I can be.
With Jesus in my Soul I have finally been set free.

Jesus Christ and Craig Harrison2011

The Lords in my eyes, now I can see . . .
The devil tried to take my life away,
But he never could ever slay me.
God has placed so much faith in my heart That I'm now finally ready
to fulfil my destiny.

𝔍𝔢𝔰𝔲𝔰 𝔠𝔥𝔯𝔦𝔰𝔱 𝔞𝔫𝔡 𝔠𝔯𝔞𝔦𝔤 𝔥𝔞𝔯𝔯𝔦𝔰𝔬𝔫2011

The thief is patient, manipulative, cunning and deceiving.
One thing I know for sure—he will never stop me Believing.
He was ready and willing to tare me apart;
But I was protected by Christ our Lord from the very start!

𝔍𝔢𝔰𝔲𝔰 𝔠𝔥𝔯𝔦𝔰𝔱 𝔞𝔫𝔡 𝔠𝔯𝔞𝔦𝔤 𝔥𝔞𝔯𝔯𝔦𝔰𝔬𝔫2011

I know in heaven that my dads shining down on me.
I regret that when he was alive, I never truly believed.
He loved us so much, and he taught me many things,
Jesus and him have helped me change everything inside of me.

Poems

In the Name of Jesus and St James,
The thief means nothing to me.
By submitting to God and resisting the devil,
Thou shall then flee.
God is all great, wonderful and almighty things . . .
Love, power and sound Mind, I will continue to sing.
Stay true to the Word; obliterate the works of the thief,
& thy shall'st leave him behind in the realm underneath.
The spirit of God, he tries to steal, kill and destroy.
Our souls, flesh and blood his demons do attack,
The Holy Ghost and God's angels are then readily deployed,
To retaliate him back.
The word is alive and active,

It is sharper than any two edge-ed sword.
Faith is the un-carnal answer,
The eternal reward from the Lord.

Praise Jesus! Jesus Christ and Craig Harrison 2011

Herbs and Coffee were created by God; they both grow out from the ground.
They have never killed a living soul, yet the one remains illegal, criminal & banned.
Alcohol I believe is the works of the enemy, created by the hands of man.
It is the 2nd root of all evil, kills hundreds of thousands, yet is legally and easily found.

Glory to God! Jesus Christ and Craig Harrison 2011

I am looking for love, there's a bride out there for me.
The Lord shall provide, so I no longer worry.
I don't care if I have to scour the entire world.
My special someone will be smart, to me pretty looking,
But most important of all, possess an awesome personality.

Praise the Lord! Jesus Christ and Craig Harrison 2011

I am both privileged and blessed to have finally found God.
Christ has always been at my side, stronger than any iron rod.
In return, I regularly fall to my knees and pray.
I diligently listen to His voice, Jesus has plenty to Say.

Praise the Lord! Jesus Christ and Craig Harrison 2011

God's will is to make me a shining example of how to be.
The Lord's love is so strong; He's made it so clear for me and everyone to
     see.
I put God first, then family and friends,
Then thy neighbour, before I do money.

Praise the Lord! Jesus Christ and Craig Harrison 2011

I endeavour to live like the people in the Biblical book of acts.
It's nice to have material things, but in reality Jesus is all I need to have.

Praise the Lord! Jesus Christ and Craig Harrison 2011

Jesus and Craig's Poem:

I simply say Jesus & the devil goes away;
Christ will make sure of that, forever & a day.
I will keep true to the Word,
Stay strong in my Christian faith . . .
. . . & listen diligently to the Father . . .
. . . & what the Lord has to say.
He is I am who I am; I will be what I will be;
God will destroy the works of evil plain for everyone to see.
He'll send sin & the thief back to hell, What will be will be?
In the holy Bible does it tell?
Jesus lives eternally.
Copyright Jesus Christ and Craig Harrison 2011

Jesus and Craig's prayer:

In the name of the Father, the Son and the holy Ghost (Spirit);

(John 10:10)

The thief comes only to steal, kill and destroy.

(1 John 4:8) (2 timothy 1:7)

God is love, power and a sound Mind . . .

(Isaiah 53:5)

. . . and by His stripes we are (were) healed . . .
. . . Through the love (grace) of our Lord, in heaven, Jesus Christ.
Amen

Copyright Jesus Christ and Craig Harrison 2011

What Jesus Christ has done for me personally!

He cured me of alcoholism (given me the gift of sobriety for a start.)

1 Peter 1:13

Wherefore gird up the loins of your mind, be sober, and hope to the end for the grace that is to be brought unto you at the revelation of Jesus Christ;

He has taken every inch of bad fear out of me, (good fear being aware of dangers.)

Psalm 27:1

The LORD is my light and my salvation—whom shall I fear? The LORD is the stronghold of my life—of whom shall I be afraid?

Jesus (Yarshua) has restored my faith which was destroyed by the thief through alcohol, drugs and smoking by inciting fear inside me. I received Him and in return blessed me with an abundant life.

John 10:10

The thief comes only to steal and kill and destroy; I have come that they may have life, and have it more abundantly.

Jesus (Son of God) has renewed my mind and blessed with the mind of Christ and I am much more intelligent and wise to the world.

1 Corinthians 2:16

"For who has known the mind of the Lord that he may instruct him?" But we have the mind of Christ.

Jesus (Immanuel) has humbled me before Him.

Matthew 18:4

Therefore, whoever humbles himself like this child is the greatest in the kingdom of heaven.

He has blessed me with serenity and peace of mind.

Serenity Prayer:

God grant me the serenity to accept the things I cannot change; courage to change the things I can; and wisdom to know the difference.
I am born again.

Romans 10:9

If you declare with your mouth, "Jesus is Lord," and believe in your heart that God raised him from the dead, you will be saved.

Jesus Christ has filled me with the Holy Ghost exactly a year since baptism and now I feel on top of the world.

Acts 2:38

Peter replied, "Repent and be baptized, every one of you, in the name of Jesus Christ for the forgiveness of your sins. And you will receive the gift of the Holy Spirit.

I am now one third Jesus Christ since becoming a born again believer, subsequent baptism and now I live in His love.

1 John 4:16

We have come to know and have believed the love which God has for us. God is love, and whoever lives in love lives in God, and God lives in him (or her).

He has drastically reduced the 7 sins in me that can lead to death. Those of which are greed, gluttony, pride, envy, sloth, lust and wrath.

John 8:11

"Go now and leave your life of sin."

I am no longer angry with the world or anyone plus I no longer wish to swear.

Colossians 3:8

But now you must rid yourselves of all such things as these: anger, rage, malice, slander, and filthy language from your lips.

I now wash more frequently and take good care of my appearance which I never managed under the influence of alcohol and drugs. I no longer wish to view sexual adult material at all. I am no longer jealous of anyone, it's a wonderful feeling—I love myself but not too much, Jesus more.

Colossians 3:5

Therefore put to death your members which are on the earth: fornication, uncleanness, passion, evil desire, and covetousness, which is idolatry.

I appreciate art, Mother Nature and music on a new level I have never felt before—God's gifts to the world is art.

Psalm 89:11

The heavens are Thine, the earth also is Thine; The world and all it contains, Thou hast founded them.

Jesus (King of kings) has restored my sanity, took away my anxiety and I can handle whatever life has to throw at me better now, praise Jesus.

I Peter 5:7

Casting all your care upon Him; for He cares for you.

Jesus (God) has taught me how to command evil spirits out my mind which is spiritual warfare.

Luke 4:8

And Jesus answered and said unto him, Get thee behind me, Satan: for it is written, Thou shalt worship the Lord thy God, and him only shalt thou serve.

I no longer serve money as my master. Money is nice to have, do not get me wrong, but love I have learned is far more important, that and health. Like Jesus said to us store riches in heaven not on earth.

Matthew 6:24

"No one can serve two masters. Either he will hate the one and love the other, or he will be devoted to the one and despise the other. You cannot serve both God and Money.

I have been through a lot of physical and mental pain in my life but still it is nothing to what Jesus Christ suffered over two millennia ago. On top of flogging, ridicule and crucifixion He also bore the world's sin. I have the upmost respect and love for someone who was both God and man at the same time, hallelujah.

Isaiah 53:5

But he was pierced for our transgressions,

He was crushed for our iniquities; the punishment that brought us peace was on him, and by His wounds we are healed.

Above all, the most high Lord Jesus Christ has taught me the true meaning of eternal love.

John 13:34-35

"A new command I give you: Love one another. As I have loved you, so you must love one another. By this everyone will know that you are my disciples, if you love one another."

Our God is an awesome God He reigns from heaven above with wisdom, pow'r and love Our God is an awesome God. Rich Mullins Our God is greater, our God is stronger, God you are higher than any other.

Our God is healer, awesome in power, our God our God. Chris Tomlin

All He asks of this world is confess Him as Lord and that God the Father raised Him from the dead in three days. (Romans 10:9)

And you will be saved just like me, give me a million pounds right now and I will give it to the poor, I store riches in heaven, I am the richest and most prosperous person in the world.

All of my days I will prove that JESUS CHRIST is real and alive.

I will not die until He says my time is up and I will have the greatest honour and privilege a man can ever receive to kneel at my Master's throne and say I love you Lord, God almighty King Yarshua.

The King of kings, Lord of lords and my best friend has commanded me to tell the world to follow Him, do not look back and SIN NO MORE.

Psalm 23:4

Yea, though I walk through the valley of the shadow of death, I will fear no evil: for thou art with me; thy rod and thy staff they comfort me.

Christ, Jesus has healed me of manic depression, obsessive compulsive disorder, alcoholism, pride, wrath, envy, sloth, greed, gluttony and lust and rescued me from three failed suicide attempts.

Jesus (Lord) has promised me a Spanish speaking bride who is beautiful both on the inside and outside in Israel and God keeps His promises.

I feel like running, skipping, praise the Lord for what He has done for me, He has set my spirit free.

I have zero fear other than for Him, He has told me to stop smoking when He orders me too and I am finally set free of evil, wickedness, and the thief and his lies. I have gone toe to toe with him on many occasions and beat him every time with Jesus.

You do not have to win every round to win a boxing match and with Jesus Christ in my corner we will knock the enemy out for good!!!!!!!

Shout to the Lord, all the earth, Let us sing
Power and majesty, praise to the King;
Mountains bow down and the seas will roar
At the sound of Your name.
I sing for joy at the work of Your hands,
Forever I'll love You, forever I'll stand,

Nothing compares to the promise I have in You. Chris Tomlin It is finally time for all the churches who worship Jesus as Lord in the world to pull together and prepare ye the return of the LORD, God almighty JESUS CHRIST.

Revelation 2:7 He who has an ear, let him hear what the Spirit says to the churches. To him who overcomes, I will give the right to eat from the tree of life, which is in the paradise of God.

My Redeemer lives, He is omnipotent (a power that can not be measured) and omnipresent (He is everywhere, sees everything and knows everything). There is no hiding place from the Father of creation as Bob Marley once told us.

Romans 10:13

"Everyone who calls on the name of the Lord will be saved."

If you get born again as He commanded, your spirit becomes identical to Him who created you. You will become one third Jesus Christ and through baptism the power of the Holy Spirit will regenerate and transform you with the power of love, give you eternal life and set you free. Give me a one way ticket to Israel and I will kneel at Calvary, Golgotha and honour Him with all my heart, soul, mind and strength and I will begin to love one another as He has loved me all my life.

John 8:32

Then you will know the truth, and the truth will set you free."

God is the Father, the Son and the Holy Ghost, the last of which also goes by the name of the Holy Spirit. He dwells deep within the hearts of every believer in our Lord and Saviour Jesus Christ! The Holy Ghost that resides in me is deeply personal, treats me as an individual and attends to all my heavenly requirements and needs.

The Holy Ghost is indeed God inside of me; I watch out and hear for Him carefully, He tells me the devil is nothing, to just say Jesus (Yarshua) rebuke you (Jude v9) and he'll soon disappear! And He is right. The enemy can only feed of my fear, I learned of a lady in Alcoholics Anonymous that the opposite of fear is faith; my faith is on fire, a fire that is burning me with the Holy Spirit right now. He spiritually warns me of any wrong doing and reveals to me the best course of action in all aspects of my life. I feel as though it is still me, I, Craig talking to myself, but the best possible Craig I can be.

Whenever I listen diligently to the voice within me, He guides me into becoming more righteous and more conscious and aware of my own faults and not those of others. He leads me from temptation and therefore I become less sinful in the eyes of my Redeemer, Lord, God, King Jeshua.

Mathew 26:41

41 "Watch and pray so that you will not fall into temptation. The spirit is willing, but the flesh is weak."

As I grow stronger in my Christian Faith, I feel more confident, more obedient, less tempted and therefore more able to help teach the gospel to others. Being Christian written by Stephen Alterburn and John Shore was given to me from a lovely, Godly lady from Set Free ministries, Rockdale, Sydney, Australia. This book has helped me realise that the pain, hurt, misery and suffering that people experience in this world is not anything of God's doing but all of man because of sin.

God gave us the magnificent gift of Free Will that unfortunately some men and women choose to abuse; and they use this gift for the works of evil instead of good. There is enough food on this beautiful planet of ours to feed all within it and enough water to quench everybody's thirst.

Universal love is what Jesus taught me to myself; to love not just my family and my friends but also any of my neighbours (I have no enemies nowadays). HE TAUGHT ME TO LOVE MY NEIGHBOUR REGARDLESS OF THEIR COLOUR, CREED OR WHAT CONTINENT THEIR FROM AND WHATEVER THEIR SOCIAL STANDING OR BACKGROUND, THEIR WEALTH OR WHAT THEY POSESS, THAT I DO NOT. WE ARE ALL GOD'S CREATURES WHO WALK UPON HIS BELOVED CREATION.

This I can only do through Christ in my compliance with God's Word outlined in the gospel. Now I have turned to Jesus, I communicate with Him regularly by reading the New Testament of the holy Bible. I am also now more devoted to the Old Testament as it teaches me the rules of creation. Just reading the book of Saint John alone educates me about grace and love. Saint Luke, for me, sums it up best what the meaning of true love really is:

Luke 10:27

He answered, "'Love the Lord your God with all your heart and with all your soul and with all your strength and with all your mind'; and, 'Love your neighbour as yourself.'"

Jesus responded to the man and said:

Luke 10:28

. . . "Do this and you will live."

I implore anyone to seek Christ in their lives; there is nothing to lose and only everything to gain. I am so glad I did; I have peace at last with the world.

The Father of creation and His Son Jesus Christ through the Holy Ghost; and through the friends and family He blessed me with, have taught me the true meaning of how to love and how to live. I also understand what it means to be a born again Christian and a child of Christ; I am one in Jesus' name:

Revelation 22:21

The grace of the Lord Jesus be with God's people. Amen.

These are the last words of the New Testament, peace be with you all. Apart from the Biblical words in this book, mine are not only inspired by the angels of Christ, Jesus; they wrote it for me.

Jesus walks with us, He really does abide in everyone. Yarshua can be found everywhere in this wonderful world of ours created by Lord God, almighty, You are awesome. Amen

Messages I received from the Lord's angels.

Love the Lord with all your heart, mind, soul and strength, love you neighbour as yourself like Jesus still loves us all and sin no more. Theses are the words that the Lord's angels command me to tell the entire world.

Yarshua is Lord Yarweh rebuke you Jude v9

1 cross 3 nails 4 forever All I need is air, food, water and Jesus Christ I am not religious; I have a personal relationship with God GOD IS YARWEH

Christianity is Christ Get behind me satan, the Lord rebuke you in Jesus' name, it is written Grace—the wages of sin had to be punished by eternal death in hell from the highest authority. The amazing news is Jesus became the world's sin and took the punishment for all if they believe in Him and follow Him.

God cursed the ground because of Adams disobedience Genesis 3:17

To receive Christ is to hand over your will over to His care God's healing power is working inside me today and everyday forever more Everything that Jesus offers beats what the devil (the thief) has to offer in abundance Don't be the next who's who, be the next you in Jesus Christ Faith, fitness and forgiveness,

The only addiction that does not revolve around fear is our Lord Jesus Christ GOD replaced in me alcohol and drugs with His Son JESUS CHRIST, I feel much better JUST SAY ZION

Grace is the love of the Lord God Just say it is written, cast out spiritual wickedness and then talk to the Lord, it works believe me I study at the college of knowledge of Christ Jesus our Lord An eye for eye only makes the whole world blind I more than a believer, I am His servant Mind of Christ, heart of a lion, spirit of God, strength of a centurion He that have an ear, let him hear The world and her ways do not concern me, just Jesus Be born again, be baptised and then confirmed Act in haste, repent at leisure Turn the other cheek and tolerate others but only have fear for the Lord Jesus Jesus Christ is everywhere and in every born again believer of Christ, Jesus Jesus is my best Friend who chose me, thank You merciful Lord The joy of the Lord is living inside of me I am one third Jesus Christ who 100% real and alive The most important thing you can do is love the Lord Jesus and to ask for His forgiveness I respect the Passion of the Christ I no longer fear what people think of me as long as I am living in the law of the Lord Jesus I Craig no longer wish to judge people, only God can do this The Lord acts and speaks through me to complete His works on planet earth GOD is love; it happened to me, it can happen to you

Yeah though I walk through the valley of the shadow of death, I will fear no evil for you are with me, your rod and your staff they comfort me. Psalm 23:4

For God did not give us a spirit of fear, but of power, love and a sound mind 2 Timothy 1:7

The Lord is my light and my salvation whom shall I fear. The Lord is the strength of my life whom shall I be afraid of. Psalm 27

Jesus Christ is real, He is a living and loving God. His Spirit dwells in me. I am in bliss because He has taken all the fear out of me except for Him Lord Jesus died so that we all shall live so whether we remain asleep or wake, we shall live with Him No man can love two masters, either he shall love the one or hate the other Matthew 6 24

I meditate with my best Friend Jesus who carries our yoke with me all the way Jesus is a jigsaw puzzle I want to continue to solve all my days I eat the bread of heaven and drink the blood of Christ

A man is defined by his actions as well as his words James 2:17

devil—d = evil God + o = good I am proud to be a servant and adopted by Jesus

Jesus not only suffered by affliction, He bore the world's sin at the same time for doing nothing wrong, imagine that and still He said forgive them Father for they know not what they do Luke 23:34

Jesus altered the chemicals of my brain to feel bliss, free and have no fear but for Him. Praise the Lord Jesus Sin miedo is no fear in Spanish I need to give blood I am not religious; I am simply one of God's servants loyal to the heavenly Father and devoted to His Son Jesus Christ. Amen Jesus is my boxing coach forever in my corner routing for me, He will not throw in the towel ever Jesus is a musical composer and a songwriter and His musical stave I read from the New testament of the holy Bible, it is beautiful and melodic In any situation just think what would Jesus do?

Get saved by Jesus Romans 10:9

My spirit is bulletproof, my dignity is unshakable, and my faith continues to grow and sprout and grow in the Lord Jesus Violence only begets more violence, stop it Jesus' name. He never used it neither shall I?

The Lord's in my eyes and now I can see Narrow minded people can not see we are all children of God, Abba Father Yarweh Jesus died on the cross to reconcile us with God and gave us the precious gift of the Holy Spirit readily available to all whom are baptised His name Find Jesus in your heart and He will illuminate it with the Holy Ghost. Thank You Father I can do all things through Christ who strengthens me Philippians 4 13

Be still and know that I am is God psalm 46:10

The opposite of fear and sin is faith in our Lord Jesus Christ The Bible tells you how to get to heaven, I trust it with every fibre in my body, you can too

Blessed are the meek, for they will inherit the earth. Mathew 5:5

Say it is written when the enemy comes knocking My biggest enemy is not the devil but me I have learned I read and hear the beauty of the gospel The enemy is a coward; Jesus is our supreme brave hero 12 minus one apostles and 70 disciples, bless them in Jesus' name You don't have to win every round to win a boxing match Father forgive me Jesus I adore Your holiness Jesus wants me to remain brave and loyal to God the Father in heaven Yarweh Jesus is the lion of the tribe of Judah I swear on my own life Jesus is Lord and I value my life now with Him nowadays Heavenly Father thank You for everything you created in 6 days Lord I come before You, I glorify your holy name. Flood over me rivers of what I need in Jesus' name. Amen

If you are angry with someone, you are only harming yourself, anger leads to hate, and then hurt, and then pain and suffering

It is wonderful to walk with the Lord's angels hallelujah
Rejoice in the King of majesty Yarshua
I have been saved by grace so have you if you desire it
I am heavenly blessed, I do not stress anymore

I appreciate all the Lord has done for me
Love one another
The day is always darkest before the dawn
Righteousness is to stand in front of God without fear of condemnation
Baptism is a commitment to GOD and a step in the right direction
My Lord has a heart of gold; words alone can not justify my love for Him
What goes around comes around Genesis 29 1- 30
Listen or thy tongue will keep thee death
Sunday morning is every morning because I found God Kurt Cobain
I am a born again Christian Praise the Lord
Alcohol IS a depressant, Jesus is the best anti depressant. Thank the Lord
Jeshua Ben Joseph
When you see sin for what it is, you do not want to do it and do not feel
    deprived of it either
I am more than a believer; I am a child of Christ
I am not alone anymore for eternity
All aboard the glory bound train
If you want God, believe in Jesus
Let go and let God
I and I
The word Christ means the anointed One
Virtue is power
Empty vessels make the most noise
A still tongue rules a wise head
Just give Jesus a go
I do not want to sin anymore
Life and death is in the power of the tongue Proverbs 18 21
Let he without sin cast the first stone John 8 7
Don't you worry about a thing?
I do not swear anymore, it limits my vocabulary
The Lord saith I am Alpha and Omega, nothing after me
Cleanliness is Christ like
You are beautiful and God's creation
Don't worry be happy
I am on the right path; I will try not to stray from now on
I need to decrease so He increases
God bless in Jesus' name

I choose to honour Jesus
I choose to honour Jesus
To serve Him all my days
Christ delivered me from evil
And took my addictions all away

God is all powerful
Our only supreme living hope
He resurrected His begotten Son
Through the power of the Holy Ghost

Christ Jesus will never let me down
Leave, hurt or stop loving me
His goodness holds no boundaries
A Spirit alive for all eternity

I choose to honour Jesus
Leave my old wicked ways behind
I worship Him every morning
Every day and every night
His love flows inside of me
Until the end of time

God is love

1:1

𝕿here's something inside so strong, Jesus lives in me, 𝕳e is not a lie.

1:2

How will I know if He really loves me?
I do not solely believe anymore, I know He is real.

1:3

God knows I am His now. The thief, the enemy and the father of lies had me long enough; no longer does it strangle or choke me.

1:4

Jesus has the whole world in His hands.

1:5

Jesus is the Son of God who created music. I dance to His songs for inspiration from now until the end of time. He is the Lord of the dance, no mistaking.

1:6

I am not afraid of expressing fear for his true rhyme, I fear Jesus who is Lord, God.

2 Timothy 1:7

For God did not give us a spirit of fear, but of power, and of love, and of a sound mind.

1:7

His infinite love will turn this world around; the light of Jesus will shine on us forever and a day.

Chapter 2

2:1

In this life, there are angelic and demonic forces, choose wisely which thou follow.

2:2

I am alive and proof there is a living God.
His name is Jesus Christ and He is Lord.

2: 3

Jesus is in most religion and the world and is the truth, the light and the way to eternal life, there is no other way.

2: 4

He is God and the Word of the holy Bible.

2:5

Art and creativeness are His gifts;
He shares all His gifts amongst man and woman on this earth especially art.

2:6

Art and music is guidance on how to get set free, and a chance to prove your love to Christ in song.

2:7

Jesus is an inspiration to a generation.

2:8

He Lives and loves every little thing.

Chapter 3

3:1

I am not thee but I know of God's name;

Exodus 3:14

God said to Moses "I Am who I Am". (Yarweh)

3:2

Wicked spiritual forces are real, speak the words of Jesus and scatter them in fear.

3:3

Sin created money and alcohol; they are therefore the roots of all evil and sin in this world.

3.4

Abstinence from the thief and sin is key.

3.5

God created herbs to eat of
. . . love, peace and serenity.

3:6

I trust in and consume what the Lord, God created.
But of man, I do not.

3:7

The enemy believe he hath mental health in his hands.
I saith he does not, Christ does.

3.8

Cleanliness is Christ like.

3:9

Burdon, regret and resentment, Christ will clean therefore of.

3.10

You are God's creation, not that of the enemy.

3.11

Therefore you are beautiful, and not ugly.
Hallelujah.

3.12

The Lord saith, I am the one, nothing after Me. If Christ (God) can't do it, it can't be done.

Chapter 4

4:1

The world today thinks it revolves around money.
It is a lie.

4:2

The Word of God is true and is law and is holy.

Hebrews 4:12

The word of God is alive and active.

It is sharper than any two edged sword.

4.3

Jesus is like a genie in a lamp, rub him the right way by reading, accepting and believing the truth. He will be released and He will make an awesome, positive impact on anyone's life. His angels will minister from then on.

4.4

The Lord saith do not forget your Maker, creator of the heavens and the earth and the sea (the universe in 6 days and rested on the 7th).

4:5

More money means more problems from the thief, however the love of Christ is free and it is plentiful.

Matthew 6:25

No one can serve two masters. Either he will hate the one and love the other, or he will be devoted to the one and despise the other. You cannot serve both God and money.

4:6

When the thief attacks your spirit, simply say . . . Jesus?
He will then go away, you just frightened it.

4.7

Why fear when the sun rises;
and tells us we are free.

Chapter 5

5:1

The Lord and life is love, nature, wildlife, and people and places . . . not money, serve Him instead.

5:2

Jesus (Lord and God) said you shall know the truth and it shall set you free. We tear down every idol.

5:3

It is written, in the holy Bible, Jesus is Lord. He is I will be what I will be, I am who I am.

5.5

Art is a gift from God, only He created it. The thief through the media endeavours to sabotage the good works of Jesus Christ.

5.6

God is love—one love, one world, one religion.
Christianity is Christ.

5:7

Yarshua's currency is faith in the one and only Lord, God that is the Holy Trinity of the Father, the Son and the Holy Spirit.

5:8

The Holy Ghost bore the virgin Mary a child who gave birth to our Lord and Saviour JESUS CHRIST!!!!!!!

Chapter 6

6:1

All Nations will return to mount Zion, Israel.

6:2

We have all sinned apart from Jesus and our Father who is the Son of man, Son of God, blessed Redeemer, holy, holy, holy Lord, God, almighty; which was, and is, and is to come . . .

6.3

. . . No wonder the enemy is frightened of by the very mention of the word . . . . Jesus. (His Father is Yarweh)

6.4

We are living in the last book of revelation GOD IS REAL . . . .

6:5

. . . Praise the Lord Jesus Christ and Yarweh, Lord of lords, King of majesty who gives life to everyone.

6:6

The Lord also gives eternal Life to anyone who chooses to accept him as their Lord and OBEY HIM!

Chapter 7

7:1

I have experienced a sample of the wrath of God and the thief; the Lord is infinitely far more powerful . . .

7:2

. . . He left me trembling; I am not worthy to speak to the Father Yarweh, only His Son Jesus and I Repent. I am no longer scared of the enemy (it) or anyone but God.

7:3

The thief can only operate in these earthly realms and not in heaven.

7:4

The Lord commands me to tell the world to turn away from sin or face his awesome wrath!

James 4:7

Submit yourselves therefore to God, Resist the Devil and he shall flee.

Chapter 8

8:1

God's wrath frightened the living day lights out of me, I have never needed Jesus so much and I do not want to go to hell.

John 3:16

For God so loved the world that he gave his only begotten son, that if whoever believes in him will not perish, but have everlasting life.

8:2

Yarshua (Lord of the earth) tells me not to surrender to the 7 deadly sins anymore:
They are pride, greed, gluttony, envy, lust, sloth and wrath . . .

8:3

. . . resist these seven, praise Jesus, then the kingdom of God can truly be yours from mount Zion and heaven.

Chapter 9

9:1

I have learned to love God first and His Son Jesus, then the Holy Ghost, then thy neighbour including family and friends before myself.

9:2

God is the greatest love of all.

9:3

There can be miracles when you believe in our Lord Jesus Christ.

9:4

It is a miracle I am still alive, I am part of God's almighty plan. Jesus heals all, He lives inside me and the word of the New Testament holy Bible is True, every word of it.

9:5

God the heavenly Father and Christ make the world go around, not money as some would make you believe . . .

9:6

Lord of lords Jesus YARSHUA died so that we may live without fear.

2 timothy 1:7

For God did not give us a spirit of fear, but of power and of love, and of a sound mind.

9:7

Jesus commands me to live life abundantly, but to turn away from sin and live by His commandments outlined in the gospel. I once thought this was impossible but it is not, I was wrong, and when I make a mistake, I simply repent.

Luke 1:37

For with God, nothing shall be impossible.

John 14:15

If you love me, keep my commandments.

Chapter 10

10:1

I am humbled by the Lord, only He is holy, righteous and without sin.

10:2

The greed and sin of man has fuelled the Lord's epic rage And I experienced a hairline sample of the wrath of God. This is another reason behind this testimony.

10:3

The natural disasters the world face are because of the sin of man.

10:4

The presence of the enemy and his influence of sin tempt civilisation and are killing the world.

John 10:10

The thief comes only to steal, kill and destroy.

I have come that they may have life and have it more abundantly. I am the good Sheppard, the good Sheppard lays down his life for his sheep.

10:5

I have learned the hard way just how precious life is and now I know Jesus, I really do know how to love.

1 john 4:8

Whoever does not love, does not know God, for God is love.

One Love

Mark 8:35

For whoever will save his life shall lose it;

But whoever shall lose his life for my sake and the Gospels, the same shall save it.

Chapter 11

11.1

I am a part of God's plan and the revelation of Jesus Christ.

11:2

Mindless drunken violence and anti social behaviour is a needless sin, saith the Lord.

11:3

I have a new life in the Lord and He has given me a purpose of which to live by, all can also do this.

Just call on His mighty name JESUS.

11:4

The saying goes; actions speak louder than words.
The Lord saith, act out the Gospel, work hard at it and speak out his words and defeat the enemy.

11:5

I can hear Bible prophecy happening to me. I feel the Lord Jesus Christ over flowing energy, it is awesome.

11.6

For all sinners should come to Jesus, and even so, all shall be saved. No matter their religion, faith or sexuality, their righteous new way shall be paved by Jesus who is God over the entire universe.

11.7

Burn down every idol that is not of Him in Jesus' name.

Chapter 12

12:1

My body is a temple on loan from God's library. I would not purposefully tear a book so I shouldn't forsake my health either.

12.2

A healthy mind starts with a fit body. I have the mind of Christ so I should take care of my body, I have give it a battering but nothing compared to what the body of Jesus Christ went through . . .

Isaiah 53:5

But he was wounded for our transgressions; He was bruised for our iniquities. The chastisement of peace was upon him and with his stripes we are healed.

12.3

The Lord only asks of us for one days worship a week for His sacrifice, it is so important what the actual day is. I worship Him everyday from the minute I wake up to the minute I sleep and do it all again the next day in Jesus' name.

Chapter 13

13:1

He or she who does right for Jesus' cause, in His eyes will they be seen. What he or she hath done for Him, they will have done back extensively, saith the compassionate, merciful loving Lord.

13:2

I have had a vivid encounter with Saint Paul. He pushed his thumbs directly into my eyes and now I can really see the truth.

John 8:32

Then you will know the truth, and the truth will set you free.

Revelation 22:13

I am alpha and omega, the beginning and the last.

Last words of the Holy bible:

Revelation 22:21

The grace of our Lord Jesus Christ be with you all. Amen.

Chapter 14

14:1

I may be young in my Biblical knowledge, but my faith is on fire.

14:2

I am preparing ye the way and return of the Lord.

John 1:23

. . . make straight the way of the Lord, . . .

14:3

Jesus and his Holy Spirit happened to me,

It can happen to you.

14:4

Sing and speaketh softly from the heart, for from the mouth does corrupt a man.

𝔐athew 15:11

𝔑ot that which goeth into the mouth defileth a man;

𝔅ut that which cometh out of the mouth, this defilith a man.

14:5

Jesus was not a soft person; He was an extremely powerful person with a soft humble, loving approach to mankind who did not deserve Him because of sin.

14:6

He is the Rabbi, the Master, the Messiah, the Christ, the King of Israel; He is God.

14:7

We all have God given talents, no person is better than any other. We are all equal and all fall short of the glory of God because we are all sinners.

14:8

God is Beautiful.

Chapter 15

15:1

I am just a speckle of sand compared to Jesus Christ, a drop of water from one of God's many oceans created by the heavenly Father, hallelujah.

15:2

God, His Son and the Holy Ghost make the world go around, not money.

15:3

I and I.

15:4

I confess my sins, declare that Jesus Christ is Lord and I ask him to forgive me of all my iniquities.
Praise God

15:5

Yarshua's light. It is powerful and awesome and God.
Thank You Lord

15:6

JESUS CHRIST

15:7

I have nothing yet I have everything.

15:8

The Lord died on the second tree.
My Redeemer lives.

15:9

To live with JESUS is to live without fear.

15:10

I follow the Lords righteous path from now until the end of time. When I sin, I will repent. I serve God as my Master not money!

John 7:38

He that believeth on me, as the scripture hath said, out of his belly shall flow rivers of living water.

Chapter 16

16:1

The world as it is today makes you believe it revolves around money. The truth is it revolves around God and his eternally loving son Jesus Christ.

16:2

Jesus lives.

16:3

My Lord, blessed Redeemer has rewarded me for passing my trials and tribulations. He has set for me FREE. I feel amazing because I have the Holy Spirit inside me, you can too.

Thank you Immanuel, (God is with us)

16:4

God is a DJ

16:5

Art is a tool GOD uses to communicate with the World.

16:6

If you believe your sick, you will be, don't in Jesus' name.

16:7

Angels and demons are real, God bless the church and the queen. Praise the Lord.

16:8

God is real, praise Jesus of Nazareth resurrected by our heavenly Father.

John 2:19

Destroy this temple and I will rebuild it in three days.

Chapter 17

17:1

I Love God and every living thing on this planet.
Praise the Lord of love, Jesus Christ.

17:2

The blood of Christ has our sins, go to Him and find out for yourself.

17:3

Jesus picked me up, turned me upside down and radically shook me so that the loose change of sin in my pockets was emptied and set me free. Thank You Lord.

Praise the Lord, King of majesty, Jesus Christ, Son of man and Son of God.

Mathew 23:26

First clean the inside of the cup, so that the outside also may become clean.

17:4

If it is not sinful or a transgression, I just do it.
God save us all.

Chapter 18

18:1

I am proud of the fact that I believe and Love Jesus Christ and I can not wait until He returns to this world and save it.

18:2

Art and creativeness is just the size of a tear drop compared to the power of God.

18:3

I have the Holy Ghost, give me all the drugs, all the money, alcohol and treasures of this world and I will humbly give them back in Jesus' name.

18:4

I know what heaven feels like in my mind, it is beautiful, it is the Holy Spirit.

18:5

I will visit mount Zion in Israel; Where Moses first received the Ten Commandments given to him by God.

18:6

God bless His Son Jesus Christ for saving me and everyone and everything in the world. It was created in seven days by I am who I am, God, almighty and Lord. Hallelujah.

John 3:16

For God so loved the world, that he gave his only begotten Son, that whosoever believeth in him should not perish, but have everlasting life.

Chapter 19

19.1

Jesus is not soft, He is the toughest there is, and He is God.

19.2

Princess Dianna is beautiful.

19.3

The world is heading towards one Religion; according to revelation Jesus will return one glad day in the very near future. We are all descendants of Abraham, King David and Jesus Christ (Yarshua).

19.4

I truly believe everything happens for a reason, we are in the Last days of the 66th book of the holy Bible that is the revelation of JESUS CHRIST!!!!!!!

19.5

The victims and their families and friends of September 11th and every other terror attack I pray for; I do not wish to ponder about evil religious extremism.

19.6

Only God has the right to judge others not man.

19.7

Sow a seed in season and watch it grow.

19.8

Non believers should give Jesus a go; they have nothing to lose and everything to gain.

19.9

The thief attempts to control the world with fear using the media as his biggest tool to tempt the world with sin.

20.20

Jesus tells me "just call on His glorious heavenly name and He will be there any time, day or night."

Conclusion

I verily know that the Christ, YARSHUA (GOD) and the devil exist. The Lord gives me guidance to keep on the righteous path. The father of lies and the enemy set traps for me along my journey.

I have seen YARSHUA'S light and felt God's wrath, Jesus opened my eyes to sin and more importantly the truth.

The trap door to satan's lair is sin; envy, lust, gluttony, wrath, sloth, pride and greed!

I was a perpetrator of all these, no more, I repent when I do. Jesus stripped me of all of them.

Overall the thief controlled my life with fear, now with God in my life, I am no longer scared of him; No fear!

The very word Jesus (Yarshua) scares him away like the coward he is. He tempted our Lord Jesus only after he fasted 40 days, what a coward and still failed.

The only one I fear is God, not man and certainly not him downstairs.

I have been blessed by Christ with the Holy Spirit, much higher than he could ever get me.

Money, alcohol, sin and unholy man are the root of all evil.

Jesus lives in me and I obey him.

I ask myself now in times of trouble what He would do if He were here right now.

DESTROY SIN AND RESTORE THIS WORLD TO IT'S FORMER BEAUTY.

I LOVE OUR LORD JESUS CHRIST

+++

GOD is one LOVE

Revelation from Jesus Christ

Water giveth Life; you can not stop it; however hard you try,
It will reach its destination.
I am honoured to have received CHRIST'S eternal blessing and He makes me
*   want to get down and pray.*
JESUS Commands me to tell the World we are running out of Chances.
By hearings his words in the gospel of the New Testament & obeying them, we
*   may find peace with God and Repent.*

Romans 1:16

I am not ashamed of the Gospel

My name is Craig Thomas Harrison and I know the truth.
I have discovered what I have been missing all my Life.
JESUS CHRIST is real and He Lives.
He Has Carried Me All my Life.
I am not sick anymore, He Has healed me.
His angels minister for me nowadays, and they have released me from my
*   burden of sin.*
All I had to do was repent and obey the Ten Commandments Given to Moses
*   from God on Mount Sinai and added to by our Lord JESUS.*
God is ready and willing to heal the entire world if only they let Him.
I had to first find in my heart and soul, how to receive His eternal love and
*   spirit of His Holiness.*
I discovered it was the cross all along.
My life is now wonderful with the knowledge that He is the World.
He walks on the ocean and leaves His footprints in the Sand.
His stars collide to give life to everyone all the time, Thanks to the cross.
I surrender to his never ending mercy stored upon me and us all, the day He
*   died on the cross over two millennia ago.*
He is the circle of life and He rules all nations.
His blood Has covered our sin and healed us, go to Him and find out for
*   yourselves.*
Jesus paid the ultimate sacrifice for the good of mankind and the world.

His everlasting candle never burns out and lights up the earth we walk upon.
He descended from the stars straight into the accepting arms of plant earth.
His gift of Mother Nature is the 2nd most important thing in life we should cherish, not money.
It took me some time, in fact a lifetime to realise everything He did that day He died, He did for me, you and everyone He sees.
He also sees all; He reminds me of my sins, I repent in His holy name.
The Lord is omnipresent meaning present everywhere.
He has just informed me He wants me off smoking soon too; He has already cured me of drinking, drugs, Bi Polar, o.c.d and lust. Praise God.
He will not let the sun go down on us until we are given the opportunity to be saved and set free again in Jesus' name, this testimony I believe, can help.
We can do this by confessing Him as Lord, asking forgiveness of our sins and then obeying His word.
I marvel at everyone of His good deeds, I owe Him this much at least since He saved me through set free ministries, Rockdale, Sydney Australia last year. Also Alcoholics anonymous continues to encourage its members to come closer to God. Bless them and I give praise to the Lord Jesus Christ once more, I am indebted to all He gave me. Praise God.
His light shines down from Heaven on all nations and is true prosperity.
Through His Gift of Music, He selects songs on the radio for me and on my MP3 player or PC and Stereo. I just embrace what He is doing and listen intently and write what He is communicating to me in the lyrics sang. He tells me to tell the World:
"What have I got to do to make you love me, to want me?
What have I got to do to be heard?"
Sorry may seem like the hardest word, but I have discovered to <u>Repent</u> To the Lord, God, almighty as the most important thing you can do on planet earth.

John 1:1

In the beginning was the word, and the word was with God and the Word was God.

I want to run to the Word to keep me safe from sin and remain with you—Jesus, gentle, graceful and merciful Lord in heaven.
JESUS CHRIST IS REAL AND HE LIVES AND SOON RETURNS!!!!!!!
Amen to us all

Comments and feedback

Craig
This is a very inspiring and detailed testimony full of the Word of God Craig. I pray that it be used to set many captives free in the name of Jesus. To free those who are still caught in addictions as you and I once were. You are truly a new creation and all things have passed away!
Praise God!

Thanks for sending me the book mate, I reckon I'm about half way through it and it's a hell of a ride, you've been to some darker places than you ever told me about, I hope that those days are well and truly behind you mate and you can channel your new found faith through that fine fender bass and maybe inspire a bunch of people in some way. Can't wait to read the rest of the book, see if you make it out of Australia! . . . . hang on, of course you did.

Great words you are quoting here Craig. And in the previous email also. Keep up the good work. "He who has begun a good work in you will perform it until the day of Jesus Christ." Blessings

Hi Craig Read the first half last night . . . . Wanted to finish it but had to go to bed! Its amazing dude so glad you know the truth and the way! Because everything Jesus said is absolute truth! Gonna read the second half now.

Something that might interest you . . . I notice that you recognise that gods name is 'I AM'. Fully it is 'I am who I am". It has actually been slightly amended due to various translations over the years but our fathers real name is 'I will be what I will be'

Pretty cool huh?
I + Will = Being

The equation of creation Catch ya later bro

Well said, Craig. You're talking truth now. Trusting you are well. Blessings

Hi Craig—It's a moving testimony you have sent. All I can say is stick to Jesus. He saved you to serve Him. Keep on with a local fellowship. Glad you completed the AA. Blessings

Hi Craig—Thank you for your latest emails. It's heartening to know you are powering on with God, and it seems He has given you a gift for writing. You might be able to use that on the Internet. Some of the set free people will be reading your longest email. Blessings

More great revelation Craig, I can agree with you that in Jesus' Name you are an evangelist to your generation, carrying the message that although the world seems without hope that Christ died for the sins of the world and that all that call on the Name of the Lord will be saved. Read Mark 16 and see there the Lord's commission to all of us believers, to go into the entire world etc

Hi Craig,
That's a powerful testimony, and one which I pray will bring others to Christ.

References and Recourses

God
Jesus Christ
The Holy Spirit inside of me
The Bible
My entire family living and in heaven
All my true friends
Wikipedia—serenity prayer, Website: The voice for love—Alternative
    serenity prayer
Mary Stevenson—Footprints in the sand
Raymond C Neale—Teresa of avila nada te turba—Teresa of Jesus
Alcoholics Anonymous meetings, UK
Set free ministries, Sydney, Australia
The secret life of a manic depressive—Stephen Fry
Zion City Tabernacle

Songs that inspire me whilst writing this testimony:

Stevie Wonder—I just called to say I love you, everything he has
    wrote
Bob Marley—One love, three little birds, everything he has wrote
Jamiroquai—Too young to die, Space cowboy
Beyonce—De ja vu, Halo
Kelly Rowland—Commander
Justin Timberlake—Senorita, Girlfriend (feat. Nelly)
Incognito (Stevie Wonder Cover)—Don't you worry about a thing.
Mary J Blidge—No more Drama
Christine Aguilera—Fighter

Bob Sinclair—I feel for you
Papa Roach—Last resort
Metallica—Fade to black, everything they have wrote
The Space Brothers—Shine
Usher—Pop ya collar
Michael Jackson—Man in the mirror, every song he ever made
Rihanna—Only Girl in the world, Disturbia
50 Cent—Many men
Whitney Houston—How will I know and a load of others by her
Kanye west—Jesus walks, all of the lights
Mariah Carey—Hero, Emotions, every song she ever wrote including Hero
Maddona—Like a prayer
Disney's the lion King—The Circle of Life (real life)
Grenade—Bruno Mars
Eric Clapton—Tears in heaven, Crossroads
Shakira—Underneath your clothes (the most beautiful girl is in the world so far in my eyes)
Various Artists—Power in the blood
Jay z—encore
2pac—Letter to my unborn child, Rear view , everything he ever wrote.
Notorious Big—juicy
I'll fly away—various artists
Power in the Blood—various artists
Zion City Tabernacle band—truly awesome
P Diddy—I'll be missing you
My redeemer lives—various artists
All worship to Jesus songs
Rapture Ruckus—I believe
Dave Moore—I was lost and you found me (Jesus used this to obliterate my desire for drink and drugs, thank You so much to this young lad. Keep up the good work to him, God bless Craig Harrison)

Thank you Lord for all You have done for me and this world, I will endeavour to sin no more. AMEN